CONTENTS

Chapter 1: Wok Welcome. Your Culinary Adventure Begins

1.1. Brief history of the Wok and its unrivaled culinary influence

Venture with us, back in time, over 2000 years to the Han Dynasty of China. Here, in the cradle of ancient civilization, our adventure begins with the humble Wok. Its first purpose? A simple one, drying grains. Yet, its unique, cavernous silhouette quickly won favor among the day's cooks.

Delve into the beauty of the Wok's design. It's not just a bowl. Its concave grace was an ingenious response to a world where fuel was precious and resources scant. The Wok's form factor facilitated an even heat distribution, allowing for resource-efficient cooking. A minor detail? Perhaps. But it's in these subtleties we see the Wok's story unfold.

Fast forward through the centuries. The Wok, a simple cooking tool, has evolved. It's now a symbol, an icon that embodies the spirit of Chinese culture, the rich tapestry of their culinary tradition. Its a singular design? A stage for the myriad cooking methods that it supports. Stir-frying's swift dance, deep-frying's hot embrace, boiling's tranquil lull, and steaming's gentle whisper; all find a home in the Wok's versatile expanse, making it an irreplaceable companion in kitchens globally.Among the pantheon of cooking techniques, wok cooking shines. It's not just about its speed or the remarkable versatility it brings to the table. No, the Wok's gift for enhancing flavors sets it apart. The orchestra of high heat and brisk stirring is a culinary magic trick, preserving the intrinsic nutrients of the ingredients while conjuring a unique, charred flavor. We know this smoky, elusive taste in the culinary world as "wok hei" or the "breath of the wok." In this sensory delight, functionality intertwines with tradition, amplifying the Wok's significance in the global culinary narrative.

So, let us welcome you to this adventure, an exploration of the world through the lens of wok cooking. Prepare to be amazed and enchanted as we delve into the history, tradition, and flavors that make this culinary journey an adventure like no other.

1.2. Different Types of Woks.

Like an artist's palette, the Wok is not a one-size-fits-all tool. It takes on multiple avatars, each varied in shape, size, and material, each with unique characteristics and advantages. Enter the realm of Carbon Steel Woks: With their feather light weight, formidable durability, and remarkable heat conduction abilities, they reign supreme, particularly within the bustling environments of professional kitchens. There's a caveat - they demand seasoning. But worry not, for this is an investment that pays dividends. Over time, they evolve, developing a natural, non-stick patina, a testament to many a meal well-cooked.

Like an artist's palette, the Wok is not a one-size-fits-all tool. It takes on multiple avatars, each varied in shape, size, and material, each with unique characteristics and advantages. Next in line are the ever-reliable Stainless Steel Woks: Boasting durability and a knack for easy cleaning, these shiny knights may not conduct heat as proficiently as carbon steel or cast iron, but they more than make up for it with their practicality. Free from the need for seasoning, they offer a convenient, low-maintenance solution to the modern cook.

Venture forth to Non-stick Woks: Light as a feather and easy to manipulate; they offer a welcoming platform for beginners venturing into the world of wok cooking. While their Achilles heel is intolerant of high heat, making them less suitable for traditional wok techniques that require intense heat, they still have their rightful place in the kitchen.

Finally, we arrive at the junction of Flat or Round Bottom Woks: The traditional round bottom woks, with their exceptional heat distribution, necessitate a wok ring to perch on most Western stoves. In contrast, flat bottom woks, a more modern adaptation, sit snugly on the stove, making them a practical choice for contemporary kitchens.

Each Wok, in its unique way, brings a different flavor and technique to the grand feast that is wok cooking. The selection of the perfect Wok thus reflects your tastes, your preferred style of cooking, and the type of stove gracing your kitchen. After all, wok cooking is not just about the act of cooking; it's about the harmonious marriage of tools, technique, and personal flair.

Chapter 2: The Sorcery of the Wok: Unveiling the Essentials of Wok Cookery

2.1. Wok Choreography: Unraveling the Dance of Wok Cooking Techniques

Dare to enter the enchanting world of Wok cooking, where culinary knowledge and artistry interweave. Mastering the ballet of wok maneuvers propels your journey, with each technique embodying a distinctive rhythm and imprinting a unique signature on the ingredients. Let's dissect the secrets held by the most renowned ones:

Stir-frying: The pulsing heart of wok cooking is stir-frying, a swift ballet of ingredients searing in a scorching bath of minimal oil. Non-stop motion is vital, ensuring the heat's fair distribution and preserving the food's vibrant hues and satisfying crunch.

Deep-frying: Embrace the capacious rim of the wok, an excellent companion for deep-frying. Its unique shape facilitates uniform heat encircling the food, crafting a flawless, golden hue. The high walls of the wok play their part, too, constraining any splatter and preserving your kitchen's cleanliness.

Pan-frying: Foods craving a robust sear, like dumplings or fish, meet their match in a wok's embrace. It's generous surface area and high heat capacity can craft the desirable crust skillfully, ensuring a tender, succulent interior.

Boiling and Braising: Believe it or not, the humble wok morphs into a traditional pot! Its vast mouth enables seamless ingredient management, from simmering noodles or broth to braising meat, and the depth hosts ample liquids.

Steaming: With the aid of a bamboo steamer basket, the wok gracefully transforms into a steamer. Prepare ethereal dim sum, vegetables, or fish, ensuring an even and gentle cooking process.

Smoking: While a less frequented path, smoking in a wok unfolds flavors. This method involves sparking a petite flame at the wok's base with tea leaves, rice, and sugar. Once covered, the food drinks in the aromatic smoke, creating a sensory delight.

These techniques breathe vitality into the ingredients, spinning the raw materials into culinary gold with their textures and flavors transformation. As you walk down this wok cooking path, you'll learn how to wield each technique, adapting it to your unique style. Remember, perfection is a child of practice! So, brave kitchen explorers, let the stirring symphony of wok cooking begin!

2.2. The Alchemist's Arsenal: Unraveling the Enigmatic World of Essential Tools and Ingredients

Prepare to be entranced by the enchanting arsenal of the wok cook, where ordinary tools transform into mystical instruments of culinary magic. In addition to these, a fascinating array of ingredients steps into prominence, vowing to stimulate your palate and take your culinary creations to the next level. Behold the wondrous revelations:

Essential Tools:

The Wok: The heart and soul of this culinary odyssey, the Wok's shape is an enigma - a captivating, deep bowl, gently sloping sides, and a wide mouth that beckons ingredients to dive in. Choose your Wok wisely, for it is the key to unlocking the flavors that lie within.

The Wok Spatula: This dynamic duo - a long-handled, round-edged spatula - becomes an extension of your hand in the Wok's theater. It deftly navigates the dance of stir-frying, tossing, and flipping with ease.

The Bamboo Steamer: Akin to a fairy's wand, this versatile steamer basket creates culinary wonders. Delicate dumplings, tender vegetables, and succulent fish emerge, all kissed by the gentle caress of steam.

The Spider Strainer: A mystical web of wire mesh cradled by a long handle, the spider strainer performs the delicate act of plucking ingredients from the bubbling depths of hot oil, ensuring a safe and satisfying fry.

Chapter 3: Vegetarian and Vegan Wok Wonders

1. Tofu and Vegetable Wok"

(4 servings, 320 kcal/serving, Cooking time: 30 minutes, Proteins: 18g, Fats: 15g, Carbs: 30g)

Ingredients:

14 oz. firm tofu (400 g)

1 medium head of broccoli (180 g)

2 medium carrots (120 g)

1 large bell pepper (200 g)

3 tbsp. soy sauce (45 ml)

3 cloves garlic, minced (9 g)

2 tbsp. vegetable oil (30 ml)

Chili flakes, to taste (optional)

Salt, to taste

Cooking:

Cut the tofu into cubes, break the broccoli into florets, slice the carrots and pepper, finely chop the garlic. Using a heated wok with oil, sauté the tofu until it reaches a golden hue. Add garlic, broccoli, carrots, pepper, soy sauce, chili, and salt to the wok. Stew everything together for 15 minutes until the vegetables are cooked.

The dish is ready to be served. Enjoy your meal!

2.Curry Vegetable Wok

(4 servings, 165 kcal/serving, Cooking time: 30-35 minutes, Proteins: 6g, Fats: 6g, Carbs: 20g)

Ingredients:

1,5 heads of cauliflower (300 g)

2 medium carrots (120 g)

1 large red bell pepper (200 g)

1 cup green peas (200 g)

1 tbsp. curry powder (6 g)

1 tbsp. vegetable oil (15 ml)

Salt, to taste

Black pepper, to taste

Cooking:

Heat the wok, and add oil. Slice the cauliflower, carrots, and pepper. Fry the vegetables in the wok over medium heat. Add green peas. Add curry, salt, and pepper, and mix well. Cook for another 5 minutes. The ready dish can be served with rice or separately. Enjoy your meal!

3. Teriyaki Tofu and Vegetables Wok

(4 servings, 215 kcal/serving, Cooking time: 30-35 minutes, Proteins: 14g, Fats: 8g, Carbs: 18g)

Ingredients:

10.5 oz. of firm tofu (300 g)

1 head of broccoli (200 g)

2 medium carrots (120 g)

1 large onion (150 g)

1/4 cup of teriyaki sauce (50 ml)

1 tbsp. of vegetable oil (15 ml)

Cooking:

Cut the tofu into cubes, the carrot into thin slices, and the onion into half-rings. Warm up the wok, introduce some oil, and sear the tofu until it acquires a golden tint. Remove and set aside. In the same oil, fry the vegetables over medium heat, then add broccoli. Return the tofu to the wok, add the teriyaki sauce, and mix well. Cook for another 5 minutes. Serve the ready dish hot. Enjoy your meal!

4. Tofu and Broccoli Wok

(4 servings, 150 kcal/serving, Cooking Time: 23-30 minutes, Proteins: 12g, Fats: 7g, Carbohydrates: 12 g)

Ingredients:

7 oz. of firm tofu (200 g)

1,5 heads of broccoli (300 g)

2 tbsp. of soy sauce (30 ml)

3 cloves of garlic, minced (9 g)

1 tbsp. of fresh ginger, minced (15 g)

1 tbsp. of vegetable oil (15 ml)

Cooking:

Cut the tofu into cubes, and divide the broccoli into florets. In a wok heated over medium heat, fry the tofu until golden, then place it on a plate. In the same wok, fry the broccoli with garlic and ginger, then add soy sauce. Return the tofu to the wok and simmer everything together for another 5 minutes. Serve the dish hot. Enjoy your meal!

5. Udon Noodles with Vegetables

(4 servings, 320 kcal/serving, Cooking Time: 35 minutes, Proteins: 10g, Fats: 6g, Carbohydrates: 56g)

Ingredients:
4 cups of Udon noodles (400 g)
1 medium carrot (100 g)
1 large bell pepper (120 g)
0,44 lbs. of broccoli (200 g)
3 tbsp. of soy sauce (or 45 ml)
2 tbsp. of vegetable oil (30 ml)

Cooking:
Prepare the Udon noodles as per the guidelines provided on the package. Cut the carrot into thin strips, the bell pepper into slices, and divide the broccoli into florets. Fry the vegetables in the heated wok with vegetable oil until soft, then add the soy sauce. Incorporate the cooked noodles into the wok and sauté the mixture for an additional 5 minutes.
Serve the dish hot. Enjoy your meal!

6. Tofu with Mixed Vegetables

(4 servings, 300 kcal/serving, Cooking Time: 30 minutes, Proteins: 15g, Fats: 12g, Carbohydrates: 33g)

Ingredients:
10.5 oz. firm tofu (300 g)
 6.5 cups of mixed vegetables, including broccoli, carrot, pepper, onion (500 g)
3 tbsp. of soy sauce (45 ml)
2 cloves of garlic, minced (10 g)
2 tbsp. of vegetable oil (or 30 ml)
Salt and pepper to taste

Cooking:
Cut the tofu into cubes and fry in a wok with vegetable oil until golden. Add minced garlic and vegetables to the wok. Stir fry until the vegetables are soft. Dress with soy sauce, season with salt and pepper to taste. Stir fry for another 2-3 minutes. Serve the dish hot. Enjoy your meal!

7. Tofu with Zucchini

(4 servings, 310 kcal/serving, Cooking Time: 30 minutes, Proteins: 18g, Fats: 18g, Carbohydrates: 22g)

Ingredients:

14 oz. firm tofu (400 g)

1 medium zucchini (225 g)

1 chili pepper (15 g)

3 cloves of garlic, minced (15 g)

2 tbsp. of vegetable oil (30 ml)

2 tbsp. of soy sauce (30 ml)

Sesame seeds for serving

Salt and pepper to taste

Cooking:

Cut the tofu into cubes and fry in a wok with vegetable oil until golden. Add minced garlic, zucchini, sliced into rounds, and chili pepper. Stir fry for another 5 minutes. Dress with soy sauce, season with salt and pepper to taste. Stir fry for another 2-3 minutes.

Serve the dish hot, sprinkled with sesame seeds. Enjoy your meal!

8. Beans and Mushrooms

(4 servings, 280 kcal/serving, Cooking Time: 30 minutes, Proteins: 13g, Fats: 8g, Carbohydrates: 40g)

Ingredients:

2.5 cups of white beans, canned or cooked, drained (400 g)

0,44 lbs. of mushrooms (200 g)

3 cloves of garlic, minced (15 g)

2 tbsp. of vegetable oil (or 30 ml)

2 tbsp. of soy sauce (or 30 ml)

Green onions, finely chopped for serving

Salt and pepper to taste

Cooking:

Slice the mushrooms thinly and fry in a wok with vegetable oil until golden. Add minced garlic and beans. Stir fry for another 5 minutes. Dress with soy sauce, season with salt and pepper to taste. Stir fry for another 2-3 minutes.

Serve the dish hot, sprinkled with green onions. Enjoy your meal!

9. Broccoli with Mushrooms

(4 servings, 150 kcal/serving, Cooking Time: 25 minutes, Proteins: 7g, Fats: 3g, Carbohydrates: 26g)

Ingredients:

2 heads of broccoli (400 g)

0,44 lbs. of mushrooms (200 g)

1 chili pepper (15 g)

3 cloves of garlic, minced (15 g)

2 tbsp. of vegetable oil (or 30 ml)

2 tbsp. of soy sauce (or 30 ml)

Sunflower seeds for serving

Salt and pepper to taste

Cooking:

Separate the broccoli into individual florets and cut the mushrooms into slices. In a wok, fry the minced garlic and chili pepper in vegetable oil. Add broccoli and mushrooms, and stir fry for 10 minutes. Dress with soy sauce, season with salt and pepper to taste.

Serve the dish hot, sprinkled with sunflower seeds. Enjoy your meal!

10. Pumpkin and Walnuts

(4 servings, 320 kcal/serving, Cooking Time: 40 minutes, Proteins: 6g, Fats: 18g, Carbohydrates: 42g)

Ingredients:

1.76 lbs of pumpkin (800 g)

1 cup of walnuts (100 g)

2 tbsp. of vegetable oil (or 30 ml)

2 tbsp. of brown sugar (or 30 g)

Salt and pepper to taste

Cooking:

Dice the pumpkin and fry in the wok with vegetable oil until tender. Add brown sugar, salt, and pepper, and stir-fry for a couple more minutes. Introduce walnuts and continue cooking for an extra five minutes, ensuring you stir regularly.

Serve the dish hot. Enjoy your meal!

11. Potatoes and Vegetables

(4 servings, 250 kcal/serving, Cooking Time: 35 minutes, Proteins: 5g, Fats: 5g, Carbohydrates: 46g)

Ingredients:

1.1 lbs. of young potatoes (500 g)
1 bell pepper (120 g)
1 medium carrot (60 g)
1 medium eggplant (200 g)
1 large onion (150 g)
2 tbsp. of vegetable oil (30 ml)
1 tbsp. of soy sauce (15 ml)
Salt and pepper to taste

Cooking:

Cube the potatoes and sauté them in a wok with oil until they turn a golden shade. Add the sliced onion, carrot, bell pepper, and eggplant. Stir fry on medium heat for 10 minutes. Dress with sauce, season with salt and pepper.
Serve the dish hot. Enjoy your meal!

12. Stewed Beans and Carrots

(4 servings, 300 kcal/serving, Cooking Time: 35 minutes, Proteins: 11g, Fats: 15g, Carbohydrates: 35g)

Ingredients:

2 1/2 cups of beans (500 g)
2 carrots (200 g)
2 tbsp. of soy sauce (30 ml)
2 tbsp. of vegetable oil (30 ml)
3 cloves of garlic (15 g)
Salt and pepper to taste

Cooking:

Heat the oil in the wok. Add minced garlic and sauté until golden. Add sliced carrots, and sauté for another 5 minutes. Add cooked beans, soy sauce, salt, and pepper. Stew all together for another 10 minutes.
Serve the dish hot. Enjoy your meal!

13. WOK with Beans and Carrots

(4 servings, 300 kcal/serving, Cooking Time: 35 minutes, Proteins: 11g, Fats: 15g, Carbohydrates: 35g)

Ingredients:

2 1/2 cups of beans (500 g)
2 carrots (200 g)
2 tbsp. of soy sauce (30 ml)
2 tbsp. of vegetable oil (30 ml)
3 cloves of garlic (15 g)
Salt and pepper to taste

Cooking:

Heat the oil in the wok. Add minced garlic and sauté until golden. Add sliced carrots, and sauté for another 5 minutes. Add cooked beans, soy sauce, salt, and pepper. Stew all together for another 10 minutes.
Serve the dish hot. Enjoy your meal!

14. Cauliflower and Curry Wok

(4 servings, 180 kcal/serving, Cooking Time: 25 minutes, Proteins: 7g, Fats: 5g, Carbohydrates: 30g)

Ingredients:

2,5 heads of Cauliflower (500 g)
2 medium carrots (200 g)
1 medium onion (100 g)
2 tsp of curry powder
1/2 cup of water (125 ml)
2 tbsp. of vegetable oil (30 ml)
Salt and pepper to taste

Cooking:

Separate the cauliflower into florets, slice the carrots thinly, cut the onion into half rings.

In a wok, over medium heat, warm up the vegetable oil. Fry the onion and carrots until golden, then add the cauliflower and curry. Mix, add the water, secure with a lid, and allow to simmer for 10-15 minutes until the vegetables have cooked through.

Add salt and pepper to taste. Serve hot. Enjoy your meal!

15. Tofu with Spinach

(4 servings, 290 kcal/serving, Cooking Time: 25 minutes, Proteins: 18g, Fats: 20g, Carbohydrates: 8g)

Ingredients:

14 oz. firm tofu (400 g)
 6 cups of spinach (200 g)
2 tbsp. of soy sauce (or 30 ml)
2 cloves of garlic (10 g)
1 tbsp. of vegetable oil (or 15 ml)
1 tsp of sesame seeds
Salt and pepper to taste

Cooking:

Cut the tofu into cubes. Mince the garlic. In a wok, over medium heat, warm up the oil, then fry the tofu until golden.

Incorporate the garlic and continue to sauté for an additional 1-2 minutes. Incorporate the spinach and soy sauce, mix, and allow to cook for an extra 2-3 minutes until the spinach has wilted.

Garnish the dish with sesame seeds prior to presenting it. Serve hot. Enjoy your meal!

Chapter 4. Seafood and Fish

1. Tomato Oysters

(4 servings, 450 kcal/serving, Cooking Time: 30 minutes, Proteins: 20g, Fats: 25g, Carbohydrates: 35g)

Ingredients:

24 oysters (400 g)

4 medium tomatoes (480 g)

4 cloves of garlic, minced (12 g)

4 tbsp. of olive oil (or 60 ml)

Salt and pepper to taste

Cooking:

Thoroughly rinse and open the oysters. Dice the tomatoes into small cubes and mince the garlic. Heat the olive oil in a heated WOK pan, followed by adding the garlic and sautéing it for a brief 30 seconds.

Add the oysters and tomatoes, sauté over medium heat for 5 minutes. Adjust with salt and pepper as per your preference, then extend the cooking process for three more minutes.

The dish is ready to be served! Enjoy your meal!

2. WOK with Octopus and Onion

(2 servings, 360 kcal/serving, Cooking Time: 30 minutes, Proteins: 25g, Fats: 10g, Carbohydrates: 30g)

Ingredients:

Octopus - 1 pc (250 g)

Onion - 2 pcs (200 g or 1 cup when chopped)

Soy Sauce - 2 tbsp

Garlic - 2 cloves (6 g)

Ginger - 1 tsp (5 g)

Olive Oil - 1 tbsp

Salt, Pepper - to taste

Cooking:

Clean, rinse, and slice the octopus into serving pieces.

Peel and slice the onion into half-rings.

In a hot WOK pan, heat the olive oil, add minced garlic and ginger, and fry for about 1 minute.

Add the octopus and onion, sauté over medium heat for 7-10 minutes, stirring.

Add soy sauce, season with salt and pepper to taste, sauté for another 2-3 minutes.

The dish is ready to be served! Enjoy your meal!

3. Vegetable Mussels

(4 servings, 400 kcal/serving, Cooking Time: 40 minutes, Proteins: 25g, Fats: 22g, Carbohydrates: 30g)

Ingredients:

1 lb. of mussels (500 g)

2 medium carrots (200 g),

2 bell pepper (300 g)

4 tbsp. of soy sauce (60 ml)

2 tbsp. of vegetable oil (30 ml)

Salt and pepper to taste

Cooking:

Rinse and open the mussels.

Thinly slice the carrot and bell pepper. Heat the WOK pan and add the oil. Sauté the carrot and bell pepper until they soften, then throw in the mussels and keep sautéing for another 2-3 minutes. In the end, incorporate the soy sauce, salt, and pepper as per your preference, and let it simmer for an additional 5-7 minutes.

There you go, your dish is ready to be served. Enjoy your meal!

4. Cilantro Tuna

(4 servings, 350 kcal/serving, Cooking Time: 20 minutes, Proteins: 40g, Fats: 10g, Carbohydrates: 15g)

Ingredients:

4 tuna steaks (700 g)

1 cup cilantro (40 g)

4 tbsp. of soy sauce (60 ml)

4 cloves of garlic, minced (12 g)

2 tsp of ginger, minced (10 g)

2 tbsp. of olive oil (30 ml)

Salt, Pepper - to taste

Cooking:

Cut the tuna into serving pieces. In a preheated WOK pan, bring the olive oil to temperature, put in crushed garlic and ginger, and sauté for approximately one minute. Add the tuna, sauté over medium heat for 3-4 minutes on each side. Introduce the soy sauce, adjust with salt and pepper as per your liking, and continue to sauté for another 1 minute.

Add chopped cilantro, mix well, and remove from heat. The dish is ready to be served! Enjoy your meal!

5. Mushroom Crab Delight

(4 servings, 380 kcal/serving, Cooking Time: 25 minutes, Proteins: 20g, Fats: 12g, Carbohydrates: 40g)

<u>Ingredients</u>:

0,88 lbs. of crab meat (400 g)

0,88 lbs. of mushrooms, (400 g)

4 tbsp. of soy sauce (60 ml)

4 cloves of garlic, minced (12 g)

2 tsp. of ginger, minced (10 g)

2 tbsp. of olive oil (30 ml)

Salt and pepper to taste

<u>Cooking</u>:

Slice the mushrooms. In a sizzling WOK pan, warm up the olive oil, toss in the finely chopped garlic and ginger, and stir-fry for around one minute. Add the mushrooms, sauté over medium heat for 5-7 minutes, until golden. Add the crab meat, sauté for another 3-4 minutes.

Incorporate the soy sauce, adjust seasoning with salt and pepper to your preference, and stir-fry for an additional 1-2 minutes.

The dish is ready to be served! Enjoy your meal!

6. Shrimp Veggie Medley

(4 servings, 320 kcal/serving, Cooking Time: 25 minutes, Proteins: 25g, Fats: 10g, Carbohydrates: 20g)

<u>Ingredients</u>:

1,3 lbs. of shrimp (600 g)

2 carrots (260 g)

2 bell pepper (240 g)

2 head of broccoli (400 g)

4 tbsp. of soy sauce (60 ml)

4 cloves of garlic, minced (12 g)

2 tsp. of ginger, minced (10 g)

2 tbsp. of olive oil (30 ml)

Salt and pepper to taste

<u>Cooking</u>:

Clean and rinse the shrimp. Slice the carrot and bell pepper into straws, and divide the broccoli into florets. In a heated WOK pan, bring the olive oil up to temperature, introduce finely chopped garlic and ginger, and stir-fry for nearly 1 minute. Add the shrimp and vegetables, sauté over medium heat for 5-7 minutes, stirring. Infuse the dish with soy sauce, add salt and pepper to suit your palate, and maintain the stir-frying process for another 2-3 minutes.

The dish is ready to be served! Enjoy your meal!

7. Salmon and Broccoli Pairing
(4 servings, 500 kcal/serving, Cooking Time: 30 minutes, Proteins: 35g, Fats: 25g, Carbohydrates: 20g)

Ingredients:

1,3 lbs. of salmon fillet (600 g)

2 head of broccoli (400 g)

4 cloves of garlic, minced (12 g)

2 tsp of ginger, minced (10 g)

4 tbsp. of soy sauce (60 ml)

2 tbsp. of olive oil (30 ml)

2 tbsp. of lemon juice (30 ml)

Salt and pepper to taste

Cooking:

Cut the salmon into small pieces, and divide the broccoli into florets. Heat the olive oil in a hot WOK pan. Add the minced garlic and ginger and sauté for about 1 minute. Add the salmon and sear it on each side over medium heat for 2-3 minutes. Add broccoli, soy sauce, and lemon juice. Season with salt and pepper to taste. Stir everything together and cook for another 5 minutes. The dish is ready to be served! Enjoy your meal!

8. Broccoli and Squid Stir-Fry

(4 servings, 300 kcal/serving, Cooking Time: 25 minutes, Proteins: 28g, Fats: 8g, Carbohydrates: 25g)

Ingredients:

4 squids (600 g)

2 heads of broccoli (400 g)

4 tbsp. of soy sauce (60 ml)

4 cloves of garlic minced (12 g)

2 tsp. of ginger, minced (10 g)

2 tbsp. of olive oil (30 ml)

Salt and pepper to taste

Cooking:

Clean, rinse, and slice the squid into rings. Divide the broccoli into florets.

Within a heated WOK pan, warm up the olive oil, introduce finely chopped garlic and ginger, and sauté for roughly 1 minute. Add the squid, broccoli, and sauté over medium heat for 5-7 minutes, stirring. Introduce the soy sauce, adjust with salt and pepper according to your preference, and continue sautéing for an extra 2-3 minutes.

The dish is ready to be served! Enjoy your meal!

9. Shrimp Noodle Extravaganza

(4 servings, 400 kcal/serving, Cooking Time: 30 minutes, Proteins: 25g, Fats: 10g, Carbohydrates: 50g)

Ingredients:

0,88 lbs. of shrimp (400 g)

3 cups of rice noodles (300 g)

4 tbsp. of soy sauce (60 ml)

4 cloves of garlic, minced (12 g)

2 tsp. of ginger, minced (10 g)

2 tbsp. of olive oil (30 ml)

4 stalks of green onions (60 g)

Salt and pepper to taste

Cooking:

Peel and rinse the shrimp. Immerse the rice noodles in hot water for a duration of 10 minutes, followed by draining them.

In a heated WOK pan, warm the olive oil, introduce the finely chopped garlic and ginger, and stir-fry for roughly one minute. Add the shrimp and sauté over medium heat for 5-7 minutes, stirring. Incorporate the noodles and soy sauce, adjust the seasoning to your liking with salt and pepper, blend everything and continue cooking for another 2-3 minutes. Sprinkle with chopped green onions before serving. The dish is ready to be served!

10. Teriyaki Shrimp

(4 servings, 450 kcal/serving, Cooking Time: 25 minutes, Proteins: 30g, Fats: 10g, Carbohydrates: 50g)

Ingredients:

0,88 lbs. of shrimp (400 g)

1 cup of teriyaki sauce (200 ml)

4 cloves of garlic, minced (12 g)

2 tsp. of ginger, minced (10 g)

2 tbsp. of olive oil (30 ml)

4 stalks of green onions (60)

Salt and pepper to taste

Cooking:

Peel and rinse the shrimp. In a preheated WOK pan, warm the olive oil, toss in the finely chopped garlic and ginger, and stir-fry for approximately one minute. Add the shrimp and sauté over medium heat for 5-7 minutes, stirring. Pour in the teriyaki sauce, adjust the seasoning to your preference with salt and pepper, mix everything together, and allow it to cook for an additional 2-3 minutes. Sprinkle with chopped green onions before serving. The dish is ready to be served! Enjoy your meal!

11. WOK with Squid and Ginger

(4 servings, 260 kcal/serving, Cooking Time: 25 minutes, Proteins: 20g, Fats: 10g, Carbohydrates: 18g)

Ingredients:

2 lbs. of squid (1000 g)
4 tbsp. of fresh ginger grated (60 g)
4 onions (400g)
2 carrots (200g)
4 tbsp. of white grape vinegar (60 ml)
4 tbsp. of soy sauce (60 ml)
4 cloves of garlic, minced (12g)
4 tbsp. of vegetable oil (60 ml)
Black pepper and salt to taste

Cooking:

Cut the squid into rings, slice the onions and carrots, finely chop the garlic and ginger. In a hot wok with oil, sauté the onions, carrots, garlic, and ginger for 3-5 minutes. Add squid, vinegar, soy sauce, salt, and pepper to the wok. Stew everything together for 10 minutes until the squid is cooked. The dish is ready to be served. Enjoy your meal!

---

12. Vegetable Scallops

(4 servings, 450 kcal/serving, Cooking Time: 25 minutes, Proteins: 25g, Fats: 15g, Carbohydrates: 50g)

Ingredients:

1 lb Scallops (500 g)
2 bell pepper (240 g)
0,44 lbs. of mushrooms (200 g)
4 tbsp. soy sauce (60 ml)
3 cloves of garlic, minced (9 g)
1 Lemon (100 g)
2 tbsp of vegetable oil (30 ml)
Salt, pepper - to taste

Cooking:

Clean the scallops, and cut the pepper and mushrooms. Crush the garlic, and cut the lemon into wedges. Warm the oil in the WOK, introduce the garlic, and sauté it until it reaches a golden hue. Add the scallops, pepper, and mushrooms, and fry everything together over high heat for about 5 minutes.

Add soy sauce, salt, pepper, and lemon wedges, and continue to fry for another 3 minutes.

You can garnish with fresh herbs when serving. Enjoy your meal!

13. Sweet Pepper Squid

(4 servings, 400 kcal/serving, Cooking Time: 25 minutes, Proteins: 35g, Fats: 10g, Carbohydrates: 45g)

Ingredients:

1.1 lbs. of squid (500 g)

2 sweet bell peppers, deseeded and sliced into thin strips (240g each)

1 medium carrot (60g)

3 tbsp. of soy sauce (45 ml)

3 cloves of garlic, minced (9g)

2 tbsp. Juice of 1 lime (30 ml)

 2 tbsp. of vegetable oil (30 ml)

Salt and black pepper to taste

Cooking:

Clean the squids and cut them into rings. Cut the sweet pepper and carrot into thin strips. Crush the garlic, cut the lime into wedges. Bring the oil to temperature in a WOK pan, toss in the garlic, and stir-fry until it becomes golden. Add the squid, pepper, carrot, and fry over high heat for 5 minutes, stirring occasionally. Add soy sauce, salt, black pepper, and lime wedges, and fry for 2-3 minutes.

Serve hot. Enjoy your meal!

14. Asian Spiced Sea Bass

(4 servings, 350 kcal/serving, Cooking Time: 25 minutes, Proteins: 32g, Fats: 10g, Carbohydrates: 30g)

Ingredients:

1.1 lbs. of sea bass fillets (500 g)

20 g Fresh ginger

2 cloves of garlic, finely minced (6 g)

1 red chili pepper (15 g)

2 tbsp. of soy sauce (30 ml)

2 tbsp. of Teriyaki sauce (30 ml)

1 tsp. of sugar (5 g)

2 tbsp. of vegetable oil (30 ml)

1 cup of white rice (200 g)

1/2 cup Green onions for serving (20 g)

Salt and black pepper to taste

Cooking:

Cut the sea bass fillet into portioned pieces. Mince the ginger and garlic, and cut the chili pepper into thin rings. In a bowl, mix the soy sauce, teriyaki sauce, and sugar, add ginger, garlic, and chili pepper. Marinate the fish in this marinade for 10-15 minutes. At the same time, cook the rice according to the instructions on the package. Heat the vegetable oil in a WOK pan, add the fish, and fry it on each side until golden. Incorporate the residual marinade into the pan, and sauté the entire mixture for an extra 1-2 minutes. Serve the fish with rice sprinkled with green onions. Enjoy your meal!

15. Mango Tiger Shrimps

(4 servings, 350 kcal/serving, Cooking Time: 20 minutes, Proteins: 25g, Fats: 15g, Carbohydrates: 35g)

Ingredients:

1.1 lbs. of tiger shrimp (500 g)

1 ripe mango (200g)

1 red onion (150g)

1 green bell pepper (120g)

2 tbsp. of coconut oil (30 ml)

2 tbsp. of soy sauce (30 ml)

1 tbsp. juice of half a lime (15 ml)

Fresh coriander leaves for serving

Salt and black pepper to taste

Cooking:

Peel the shrimp, cut the mango into thin slices, and cut the onion and green pepper into thin strips. In a WOK pan, warm the coconut oil, introduce the onion, and sauté until it turns golden. Follow up by adding the shrimp and frying each side for 2-3 minutes.

Then add the green pepper and mango, and fry for another 2-3 minutes, stirring. Add the soy sauce, lime juice, salt, and black pepper, mix well, and remove from heat. Serve immediately, sprinkling with fresh coriander. Enjoy your meal!

Chapter 5: Poultry Choices

1.Chicken and Veggie Stir-Fry

(4 servings, 550 kcal/serving, Cooking Time: 30 minutes, Proteins: 45g, Fats: 20g, Carbohydrates: 50g)

Ingredients:

1,3 lbs. of chicken fillet (600 g)

2 heads of cauliflower (400 g)

4 bell peppers (600 g)

4 cloves of garlic, minced (12 g)

4 tbsp. of soy sauce (60 ml)

4 tbsp. of olive oil (60 ml)

Salt and pepper to taste

Cooking:

Cut the chicken fillet into serving pieces. Heat the olive oil in a hot WOK pan. Add the minced garlic and sauté for about 1 minute. Add the chicken fillet and sear over medium heat for 5-7 minutes until golden. Add the bell pepper and cauliflower, then the soy sauce. Season with salt and pepper to taste. Stir and cook for another 5-7 minutes. The dish is ready to be served! Enjoy your meal!

2. Chicken and Udon Noodles

(4 servings, 680 kcal/serving, Cooking Time: 35 minutes, Proteins: 48g, Fats: 22g, Carbohydrates: 80g)

Ingredients:

1,3 lbs. of chicken fillet (600 g)

4 cups of udon noodles (400 g)

2 carrot (240 g)

4 cloves of garlic, minced (12 g)

4 tbsp. of soy sauce (60 ml)

4 tbsp. of olive oil (60 ml)

Salt and pepper to taste

Cooking:

Cut the chicken fillet into serving pieces. Slice the carrot into thin strips. Prepare the udon noodles as per the guidelines stipulated on their packaging. Heat the olive oil in a hot WOK pan. Introduce the finely chopped garlic and stir it in until it releases a noticeable aroma, a process that should take under a minute.. Add the chicken fillet and sear over medium heat for 5-7 minutes until golden. Add the carrot and the boiled noodles, then the soy sauce. Season with salt and pepper to taste. Stir everything together and cook for another 5 minutes.

The dish is ready to be served! Enjoy your meal!

---

3. Duck and Mushroom Medley

(4 servings, 600 kcal/serving, Cooking Time: 50 minutes, Proteins: 62g, Fats: 20g, Carbohydrates: 72g)

Ingredients:

1.1 lbs. of duck fillet (500 g)

0,55 lbs. of mushrooms (250 g)

1 large onion (200 g)

2 cloves of garlic, minced (6 g)

3 tbsp. of soy sauce (45 ml)

1 tsp. of sugar (5 g)

2 tbsp. of olive oil (30 ml)

Salt and pepper to taste

Cooking:

Cut the duck fillet into thin strips. Slice the mushrooms and onion.

In a bowl, blend the soy sauce and sugar together, add the duck fillet, and make sure it is thoroughly mixed in. In a WOK pan, warm up the olive oil. Add the minced garlic and sauté over medium heat for about 1 minute. Add the onion and mushrooms, and sauté for about 5 minutes. Add the duck fillet along with the marinade, and stir. Let it simmer, stirring now and then, for approximately 15-20 minutes or until the duck has reached its desired level of doneness. Season it according to your preference with salt and pepper, then give it a good stir. The dish is ready to serve. Enjoy your meal!

4. Chicken in Teriyaki Sauce

(4 servings, 600 kcal/serving, Cooking Time: 30 minutes, Proteins: 55g, Fats: 25g, Carbohydrates: 45g)

<u>Ingredients</u>:

1,3 lbs. of chicken fillet (600 g)

2 heads of broccoli (400 g)

2 carrots (240 g)

8 tbsp. of Teriyaki sauce (120 ml)

4 cloves of garlic minced (12 g)

4 tbsp. of olive oil (60 ml)

Salt and pepper to taste

<u>Cooking</u>:

Slice the chicken fillet into thin strips. Also, cut the carrot into strips and divide the broccoli into florets. Heat the olive oil in a hot WOK pan. Add the minced garlic and sauté for about 1 minute. Add the chicken fillet and sear it over medium heat for 5-7 minutes. Add the carrot and broccoli, then the teriyaki sauce. Season with salt and pepper to taste. Stir everything together and cook for another 5 minutes.

The dish is ready to be served! Enjoy your meal!

5. Chicken with Pineapple

(4 servings, 650 kcal/serving, Cooking Time: 30 minutes, Proteins: 58g, Fats: 15g, Carbohydrates: 74g)

Ingredients:

1.1 lbs. of chicken fillet (500 g)

½ of pineapples fresh or canned, (300 g)

2 large sweet peppers (240 g)

3 tbsp. of soy sauce (45 ml)

2 tbsp. of olive oil (30 ml)

1 tbsp. of sugar (12 g)

Salt and pepper to taste

Cooking:

Cut the chicken fillet into small pieces, the pineapples into cubes, and the sweet pepper into stripes. Heat up the WOK pan, and add olive oil. Put in the chicken and fry it over high heat until golden, about 10 minutes. Add the pineapple and pepper, continue frying for another 5 minutes, stirring occasionally. Sprinkle with sugar, pour soy sauce over the top, stir well. Continue to cook for another 5 minutes. Salt and pepper to taste and stir.

The dish is ready to serve hot. Enjoy your meal!

6. Turkey and Veggies

(4 servings, 550 kcal/serving, Cooking Time: 35 minutes, Proteins: 48g, Fats: 16g, Carbohydrates: 60g)

Ingredients:

1.1 lbs of turkey fillet (500 g)

1 head of broccoli (200 g)

2 large carrots (240 g)

2 large sweet peppers (240 g)

3 tbsp of soy sauce (45 ml)

2 tbsp of olive oil (30 ml)

Salt and pepper to taste

Cooking:

Cut the turkey into small pieces, slice the carrot into thin strips, cut the sweet pepper into cubes, and divide the broccoli into florets. Heat the olive oil in the WOK. Fry the turkey until golden for about 10 minutes. Add the carrot, broccoli, and sweet pepper. Continue to fry the turkey over high heat for another 10 minutes. Incorporate the soy sauce, season with salt and pepper as per your preference, and mix well.

Continue to cook for another 5 minutes.

The dish is ready to serve hot. Enjoy your meal!

7. Duck with Pineapples

(4 servings, 620 kcal/serving, Cooking Time: 40 minutes, Proteins: 42g, Fats: 22g, Carbohydrates: 75g)

Ingredients:

1,1 lbs. of duck fillet (500 g)

1 pineapple (500 g)

1 leek (130 g)

4 tbsp. of teriyaki sauce (60 ml)

2 tbsp. of olive oil (30 ml)

Salt and pepper to taste

Cooking:

Cut the duck into small pieces, the pineapples into cubes, and the leek into rings. Heat the olive oil in the WOK. Fry the duck until golden for about 10 minutes. Add the leek and pineapples. Continue to fry the duck over high heat for another 10 minutes. Incorporate the soy sauce, season with salt and pepper as per your preference, and mix well.

Continue to cook for another 5 minutes. The dish is ready to serve hot. Enjoy your meal!

8. Turkey and Veggie Mix
(4 servings, 550 kcal/serving, Cooking Time: 40 minutes, Proteins: 60g, Fats: 18g, Carbohydrates: 70g)

Ingredients:

1.1 lbs of turkey fillet (500 g)

2 bell peppers (250 g)

1 head of broccoli (200 g)

1 carrot (120 g)

2 cloves of garlic, minced (6 g)

2 tbsp. of olive oil (30 ml)

2 tbsp. of soy sauce (30 ml)

Salt and pepper to taste

Cooking:

Cut the turkey fillet into pieces. Slice the pepper and carrot into strips, divide the broccoli into florets. In a WOK pan, warm up the olive oil.

Add the minced garlic and stir, allow it to lightly brown, which will take about a minute. Introduce the turkey fillet to the pan and sauté it on medium heat for approximately 10 minutes. Add the bell pepper, broccoli and carrot, then the soy sauce.

Season with salt and pepper as per your liking, mix everything, and continue the cooking process for another 10 minutes.

The dish is ready to serve. Enjoy your meal!

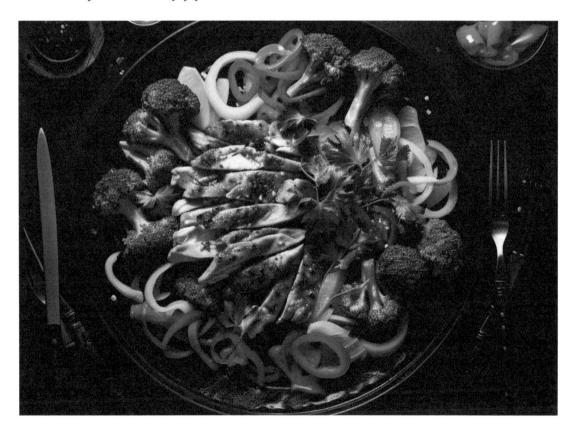

9. Chicken with Shiitake Mushrooms

(4 servings, 420 kcal/serving, Cooking Time: 35 minutes, Proteins: 30g, Fats: 11g, Carbohydrates: 50g)

Ingredients:

0,88 lbs. of chicken fillet (400 g)

0,44 lbs. of shiitake mushrooms (200 g)

2 carrots (200 g)

3 tbsp. of soy sauce (45 ml)

2 tbsp. of olive oil (30 ml)

Salt and pepper to taste

Cooking:

Cut the chicken fillet into small pieces, mushrooms into strips, and carrots into thin sticks.

Heat the olive oil in the WOK. Fry the chicken fillet until golden for about 10 minutes.

Add the carrots and mushrooms. Continue to fry the chicken over high heat for another 10 minutes. Incorporate the soy sauce, season with salt and pepper as per your preference, and mix well.

Continue to cook for another 5 minutes. The dish is ready to serve hot. Enjoy your meal!

10. Teriyaki Turkey and Veggies

(4 servings, 400 kcal/serving, Cooking Time: 30 minutes, Proteins: 35g, Fats: 8g, Carbohydrates: 45g)

Ingredients:

1,1 lbs. of turkey fillet (500 g)

1 head of broccoli (200 g)

2 carrots (200 g)

2 red bell pepper (250 g)

3 tbsp. soy sauce (45 ml)

3 tbsp. teriyaki sauce (45 ml)

1 tbsp. honey (15 ml)

2 tbsp. vegetable oil (30 ml)

2 cloves of garlic, minced (6 g)

 1 cup of rice (200 g)

Salt and pepper to taste

Cooking:

Cut the turkey fillet into small pieces. Cut the vegetables (broccoli, carrot, pepper) as you like. In a sizeable bowl, blend together the soy sauce, teriyaki sauce, and honey. Add the meat to it and mix well. Leave it to marinate for 15-20 minutes. During this time, cook the rice according to the instructions on the package. In a spacious WOK pan, warm up the oil, introduce the finely chopped garlic, and give it a brief sauté. Then add the marinated meat and fry it until it's cooked. Add the chopped vegetables and continue frying everything together for another 5-7 minutes.
Serve the finished dish with rice. Enjoy your meal!

11. Chicken with Pineapples and Cashews

(4 servings, 430 kcal/serving, Cooking Time: 30 minutes, Proteins: 30g, Fats: 15g, Carbohydrates: 45g)

Ingredients:

1,1 lbs. chicken fillet (500 g)

0,5 can pineapples (canned) (250 g)

1 onion (100 g)

1 carrot (100 g),

0,5 cup cashews (100 g)

2 tbsp soy sauce (30 ml)

2 tbsp vegetable oil (30 ml)

Salt and pepper to taste

Cooking:

Cut the chicken fillet into small pieces. Cut the onion and carrot into half rings and pineapples into cubes. Warm up some vegetable oil in a WOK and sauté the chicken until it reaches a golden hue. Season with salt and pepper. Add the onion and carrot, and fry everything together for about 5 minutes.
Then add the pineapples and soy sauce, and fry for another 2-3 minutes. At the end, add the cashews, mix well and remove from the heat. Serve hot. Enjoy your meal!

12. Chicken with Pineapples and Coconut Sauce

(4 servings, 450 kcal/serving, Cooking Time: 35 minutes, Proteins: 32g, Fats: 14g, Carbohydrates: 50g)

Ingredients:

1,1 lbs. chicken fillet (500 g)
0,6 can pineapples (canned) (300 g)
1 red bell pepper (120 g)
1 carrot (100 g)
1 can coconut milk (400 ml)
1 tsp. curry powder (5 g)
2 tbsp. Vegetable oil (30 ml)
1 cup of rice (200 g)
Salt and pepper to taste

Cooking:

Cut the chicken fillet into small pieces. Slice the carrot and pepper into slender strips. Heat the vegetable oil in a WOK pan and fry the chicken fillet until golden brown. Add the curry, stir, and continue frying for a couple more minutes. Add the carrot, pepper, and pineapples, stir, and fry all together for another 5 minutes. Introduce the coconut milk, adding salt and pepper as per your taste. Simmer everything together over medium heat for about 10 minutes. In the meantime, cook the rice. Serve the dish hot, with rice. Enjoy your meal!

13. Chicken with Peppers and Peanut Sauce

(4 servings, 420 kcal/serving, Cooking Time: 35 minutes, Proteins: 28g, Fats: 22g, Carbohydrates: 30g)

Ingredients:

1,1 lbs. chicken fillet (500 g)

1 red bell pepper (120 g)

1 yellow bell pepper (120 g)

1 leek (130 g)

3 tbsp. soy sauce (45 ml)

2 tbsp. peanut oil (30 ml)

1 tbsp. honey (15 ml)

1 tbsp. lemon juice (15 ml)

0.3 cup ground peanuts (50 g)

Salt and pepper to taste

Cooking:

Cut the chicken fillet into small pieces. Cut the peppers and leek into thin strips. Mix soy sauce, peanut oil, honey, and lemon juice in a bowl. This will be your peanut sauce.

In a WOK, warm a bit of vegetable oil and sauté the chicken until it turns a golden brown. Season with salt and pepper. Add the peppers and leek, and fry for another 5 minutes. Add the peanut sauce and ground peanuts, mix well, and fry for a couple more minutes. Serve the dish hot. Enjoy your meal!

---

14. Chicken, Spinach and Sweet Red Pepper Wok

(4 servings, 400 kcal/serving, Cooking Time: 30 minutes, Proteins: 20g, Fats: 20g, Carbohydrates: 40g)

Ingredients:

1,1lbs. chicken fillet (500 g)

1 sweet red pepper (120 g)

6 cups of spinach (200 g)

2 tbsp. vegetable oil (30 ml)

2 tbsp. soy sauce (30 ml)

2 cloves of garlic, minced (6 g)

Salt and pepper to taste

Cooking:

Dice the chicken fillet into bite-sized portions, slice the sweet pepper into strips, and mince the garlic. Warm the vegetable oil in a large WOK, introduce the chicken, and sauté until it acquires a golden brown color.

Add the sweet pepper and garlic, fry everything together for about 5 minutes, add the soy sauce, and mix. Then add the spinach, mix, and continue cooking over the fire for a couple more minutes until the spinach wilts. Salt and pepper to taste, and stir. Your WOK with chicken, spinach, and sweet red pepper is ready to serve. Enjoy your meal!

15. Duck with Oranges

(4 servings, 380 kcal/serving, Cooking Time: 45 minutes, Proteins: 25g, Fats: 15g, Carbohydrates: 35g)

Ingredients:

1.1 lbs. of duck fillet (500 g)

2 oranges (300 g)

1 carrot (100 g)

3 tbsp. of soy sauce (45 ml)

2 tbsp. of olive oil (30 ml)

Salt and pepper to taste

Cooking:

Cut the duck fillet into small pieces. Slice the oranges and carrots into thin slices.

Heat the olive oil in the WOK. Fry the duck fillet until golden for about 10 minutes.

Add the carrots and oranges. Continue to fry the duck over high heat for another 10 minutes.

Incorporate the soy sauce, season with salt and pepper as per your preference, and mix well.

Continue to cook for another 5 minutes. The dish is ready to serve hot. Enjoy your meal!

Chapter 6: Pork, Beef and lamb Perfections

1.Pork and Veggie Medley

(4 servings, 480 kcal/serving, Cooking Time: 30 minutes, Proteins: 34g, Fats: 24g, Carbohydrates: 20g)

<u>Ingredients</u>:

1,1 lbs. of pork (500 g)

1 red pepper (150 g)

1 head of broccoli (200 g)

4 cloves of garlic, minced (20 g)

2 tbsp. of vegetable oil (30 ml)

Salt and pepper to taste

<u>Cooking</u>:

Cut the pork into thin strips. Slice the red pepper into strips, and divide the broccoli into florets.

Heat the vegetable oil in the WOK. Fry the pork until golden for about 10 minutes.

Incorporate the red pepper, broccoli, and minced garlic into the pan, adjust the seasoning with salt and pepper to your taste, and continue stir-frying the blend for approximately 10 more minutes. The dish is ready to serve hot. Enjoy your meal!

2. Beef with Bamboo Shoots

(4 servings, 650 kcal/serving, Cooking Time: 40 minutes, Proteins: 52g, Fats: 32g, Carbohydrates: 22g)

Ingredients:

1,1 lbs. of beef (500 g)

1 can of bamboo shoots (227 g)

2 tbsp. of soy sauce (30 ml)

2 tbsp. of olive oil (30 ml)

4 cloves of garlic (20 g)

Salt and pepper to taste

Cooking:

Cut the beef into thin slices. Heat the olive oil in the WOK. Fry the beef over medium heat until brown, about 10 minutes. Add finely chopped garlic, bamboo, salt, and pepper to taste.

Add the soy sauce, stir well, and cook for another 5 minutes. Serve the dish hot. Enjoy your meal!

3. Pork and Mushrooms Combo

(4 servings, 580 kcal/serving, Cooking Time: 40 minutes, Proteins: 36g, Fats: 28g, Carbohydrates: 34g)

Ingredients:

1,1 lbs. of pork (500 g)

0,44 lbs. of mushrooms (200 g)

2 tbsp. of soy sauce (30 ml)

2 tbsp. of vegetable oil (30 ml)

4 cloves of garlic, minced (20 g)

Salt and pepper to taste

Cooking:

Cut the pork into small pieces. Heat the vegetable oil in the WOK. Fry the pork over medium heat until golden for about 10 minutes. Add finely chopped garlic, mushrooms, salt, and pepper to taste. Pour in the soy sauce, ensure a thorough mix, and allow it to cook for an additional 5 minutes. The dish is ready to serve hot. Enjoy your meal!

4. Tropical Lamb with Pineapples

(4 servings, 640 kcal/serving, Cooking Time: 35 minutes, Proteins: 42g, Fats: 30g, Carbohydrates: 45g)

Ingredients:

1,1 lbs. of lamb (500 g)

1/2 pineapple (300 g),

3 tbsp of sweet chili sauce (45 ml)

2 tbsp of vegetable oil (30 ml)

4 cloves of garlic, minced (20 g)

Salt and pepper to taste

Cooking:

Cut the lamb into small pieces. Cut the pineapple into small pieces. Heat the vegetable oil in the WOK. Fry the lamb over medium heat until golden for 10-15 minutes. Add finely chopped garlic, pineapple, salt, and pepper to taste. Add the chili sauce and stew everything over low heat for 15-20 minutes. Serve the dish hot. Enjoy your meal!

5. Asparagus Beef Stir-fry

(4 servings, 500 kcal/serving, Cooking Time: 25 minutes, Proteins: 25g, Fats: 25g, Carbohydrates: 30g)

Ingredients:

1,1 lbs. of beef (500 g)

250 g of asparagus

2 tbsp. of soy sauce (30 ml)

2 tbsp. of sesame oil (30 ml)

4 cloves of garlic, minced (20 g)

2 shallots, thinly sliced (60 g)

Sesame seeds for garnish

Salt and pepper to taste

Cooking:

Slice the beef into thin strips. Preheat your wok over medium heat and add the sesame oil. Sauté the meat until it turns golden, roughly 10 minutes. Introduce the finely chopped garlic, shallots, asparagus, and season with salt and pepper. Pour in the soy sauce, stir well, and let it cook for another 5 minutes. Garnish with sesame seeds just before serving. The dish is best enjoyed hot. Enjoy your meal!

6. Lamb and Broccoli Mix

(4 servings, 600 kcal/serving, Cooking Time: 35 minutes, Proteins: 39g, Fats: 35g, Carbohydrates: 26g)

Ingredients:

1,1 lbs. lamb (500 g)

1 medium head of broccoli (200 g)

2 tbsp. soy sauce (30 ml)

2 tbsp. Olive oil (30 ml)

4 cloves of garlic (20 g)

1/2 tsp. red chili flakes (to taste)

Salt and pepper to taste

Cooking:

Cut the lamb into bite-sized pieces. Heat the olive oil in the WOK. Sauté the lamb on medium heat until it turns brown, a process that should take around 10 minutes. Add chopped garlic, red chili flakes, and broccoli florets to the WOK—season with salt and pepper. Drizzle with soy sauce, mix it well, and cook for another 5-7 minutes until the broccoli is tender-crisp. Serve your dish piping hot and savor the flavors. Enjoy your meal!

---

7. Sweet and Sour Pork

(4 servings, 660 kcal/serving, Cooking Time: 50 minutes, Proteins: 38g, Fats: 32g, Carbohydrates: 40g)

Ingredients:

1.1 lbs pork (500 g)

2 sweet peppers (250 g)

0,5 can pineapples (canned) (250 g)

2 tbsp rice vinegar (30 ml)

1 tbsp sugar (15 g)

1 tbsp soy sauce (15 ml)

2 tbsp tomato sauce (30 ml)

1 tsp starch (5 g)

Vegetable oil for frying

Cooking:

Cut the pork into small pieces, sweet pepper into strips, and pineapples into slices. In a wok, warm the oil and sauté the pork until it reaches a golden hue. Add sweet pepper and pineapples, and fry for another 5 minutes. Mix vinegar, sugar, soy and tomato sauces, and starch in a separate bowl, then add the mixture to the wok. Simmer over medium heat, continuously stirring, until the sauce reaches a thicker consistency.

Serve hot, sprinkled with herbs. Enjoy your meal!

8. Pork with Pineapples

(4 servings, 420 kcal/serving, Cooking Time: 40 minutes, Proteins: 27g, Fats: 15g, Carbohydrates: 42g)

Ingredients:

1,1 lbs. pork (500 g)

1 can pineapples (canned) (500 g)

4 tbsp. soy sauce (60 ml)

1 tbsp. starch (15 g)

1 sweet pepper (200 g)

2 tbsp. olive oil (30 ml)

Salt and pepper to taste

Cooking:

Cut the pork into small pieces. Slice the sweet pepper into cubes. Heat the olive oil in the WOK. Fry the pork until golden for about 10 minutes. Add the sweet pepper. Continue to fry with the pork for another 5 minutes. Dissolve the starch in the soy sauce and add to the WOK. Add the pineapples, salt, and pepper to taste, and stir. Continue to cook for another 5 minutes. The dish is ready to serve hot. Enjoy your meal!

9. Coconut Beef Delight

(4 servings, 700 kcal/serving, Cooking Time: 50 minutes, Proteins: 40g, Fats: 38g, Carbohydrates: 32g)

Ingredients:

1,1 lbs. of beef (500 g)

1 can of coconut milk (400 ml)

4 shallots (80 g)

2 cloves of garlic, minced (6 g)

1 tsp. of grated ginger (5 g)

2 tsp. of red curry paste (10 g)

1 tbsp. of soy sauce (15 ml)

1 lime (60 g)

Cilantro, to taste

Vegetable oil for frying

Cooking:

Cut the beef into small pieces. Finely chop the onions, garlic, and ginger. Warm the oil in a wok and sauté the meat until it achieves a golden color.

Add onions, garlic, ginger, curry, and fry for 5 minutes.

Pour in coconut milk, add soy sauce, boil, and simmer for 20 minutes. Add the juice of half a lime, and stir. Serve hot, sprinkled with cilantro and a slice of lime. Enjoy your meal!

---

10. Mango Lamb Stir-Fry

(4 servings, 650 kcal/serving, Cooking Time: 40 minutes, Proteins: 36g, Fats: 30g, Carbohydrates: 38g)

Ingredients:

1,1 lbs. lamb (500 g)

1 fresh mango (300 g)

3 cloves garlic, minced (12 g)

1 red onion (150 g)

1 red chili pepper

A small bunch of cilantro (20 g)

3 tbsp. soy sauce (45 ml)

2 tbsp. vegetable oil (30 ml)

Cooking:

Cut the lamb into small mango pieces into cubes, finely chop the onion and garlic.

In a heated wok with oil, fry the lamb until golden brown. Add onion, garlic, and finely chopped chili pepper to the wok, and fry for another couple of minutes. Pour in soy sauce and add mango cubes, stew everything together for 5-7 minutes. Before serving, add finely chopped cilantro. The dish is ready to be done. Enjoy your meal!

11. Spicy Lamb Dish
(4 servings, 680 kcal/serving, Cooking Time: 40 minutes, Proteins: 40g, Fats: 32g, Carbohydrates: 35g)

<u>Ingredients</u>:

1 lbs. of lamb (500 g)
2 bell peppers (250 g)
1 medium head of broccoli (200 g)
1 carrot (120 g)
2 cloves of garlic, minced (6 g)
2 tbsp. of olive oil (30 ml)
2 tbsp. of soy sauce (30 ml)

<u>Cooking</u>:

Cut the lamb into small pieces, finely chop the onions and garlic, and cut the tomatoes into cubes. In a heated wok with oil, fry the lamb until golden brown. Incorporate onions and garlic into the wok, and sauté them alongside the meat for a few more minutes. Add tomatoes, paprika, turmeric, coriander, salt, and pepper. Stew everything together for 10-15 minutes until the meat is cooked. The dish is ready to be served. Enjoy your meal!

12. Peppery Beef Stir-Fry

(4 servings, 450 kcal/serving, Cooking Time: 30 minutes, Proteins: 32g, Fats: 18g, Carbohydrates: 35g)

Ingredients:

1,1 lbs. of turkey fillet (500 g)
2 bell peppers (250 g)
1 head of broccoli (200 g)
1 carrot (120 g)
2 cloves of garlic, minced (6 g)
2 tbsp. of olive oil (30 ml)
2 tbsp. of soy sauce (30 ml)

Cooking:

Cut the beef into thin strips. Slice the bell pepper into strips. Heat the vegetable oil in the WOK. Fry the meat until golden for about 10 minutes. Incorporate the bell pepper, minced garlic, and soy sauce, season with salt and pepper to your liking, and proceed to sauté for an additional 10 minutes. The dish is ready to serve hot. Enjoy your meal!

---

13. Pork with Curry and Mini Corn

(4 servings, 550 kcal/serving, Cooking Time: 30 minutes, Proteins: 30g, Fats: 25g, Carbohydrates: 55g)

Ingredients:

1,1 lbs. pork neck (500 g)
1 can of mini corn (300 g - 400 g)
3 cloves of garlic minced (9 g)
3 tbsp of soy sauce (45 ml)
1 tsp curry powder (5g)
2 tbsp of vegetable oil (30 ml)
Salt and pepper to taste

Cooking:

Cut the pork neck into small pieces, finely chop the garlic.

In a deep WOK, warm up the vegetable oil, introduce the pork, and sauté it until it turns golden brown. Add garlic, mini corn (drain the liquid), soy sauce, and curry, and mix well. Fry everything together for another 5 minutes to mix the flavors. Salt and pepper to taste, and stir. Your WOK with pork, curry, and mini corn is ready to serve. Enjoy your meal!

14. WOK with Lamb and Spinach

(4 servings, 480 kcal/serving, Cooking Time: 35 minutes, Proteins: 34g, Fats: 22g, Carbohydrates: 25g)

Ingredients:

1,1 lbs. of lamb (500 g)

6 cups of spinach (200 g)

4 cloves of garlic, minced (20 g)

2 tbsp of vegetable oil (30 ml)

Salt and pepper to taste

Cooking:

Cut the lamb into small pieces. Heat the vegetable oil in the WOK. Fry the lamb until golden for about 10 minutes. Add the finely chopped garlic, spinach, salt, and pepper to taste, and continue to fry for about 5 minutes or until the spinach wilts. The dish is ready to serve hot. Enjoy your meal!

15. Beef with Bamboo Shoots and Shiitake Mushrooms

(4 servings, 600 kcal/serving, Cooking Time: 35 minutes, Proteins: 35g, Fats: 25g, Carbohydrates: 60g)

<u>Ingredients</u>:

1,1 lbs. beef (500 g)

0,44 lbs. shiitake mushrooms (200 g)

1 can of bamboo shoots (300 g - 400 g)

4 tbsp. of soy sauce (60 ml)

1 tsp. sugar

2 cloves of garlic, minced (6 g)

1 piece of ginger (5 g)

2 tbsp of vegetable oil (30 ml)

Salt, black pepper to taste

<u>Cooking</u>:

Cut the beef into thin slices. If the shiitake mushrooms are dried, soak them in water for 20 minutes, then cut off the hard stems. Cut the bamboo shoots (draining the liquid) and mushrooms into thin strips. Slice the garlic and ginger thinly. In the WOK, warm up the oil, introduce the beef, and sauté until it acquires a golden brown color. Add the garlic and ginger, mushrooms, and bamboo, and fry everything together for a couple of minutes. Introduce the soy sauce, sugar, salt, and pepper, mix everything thoroughly, and proceed to sauté for an additional 5 minutes. Serve hot. Enjoy your meal!

Chapter 7: Rice, Noodles and Grain.

1. Bulgur Wheat Veggie Stir-Fry

(4 servings, 320 kcal/serving, Cooking time: 30 minutes, Proteins: 12g, Fats: 8g, Carbs: 56g)

<u>Ingredients</u>:

2 cups cooked bulgur wheat (408 g

0,5 head of broccoli (70 g)

1 red bell pepper (150 g)

2 tbsp. vegetable oil (28 g)

1/4 cup soy sauce (60 ml)

1 tbsp. minced garlic (6 g)

Salt, black pepper to taste

<u>Cooking</u>:

Heat oil in the wok. Add broccoli and bell pepper, and stir-fry until tender (5-7 mins). Stir in cooked bulgur, and mix well (2-3 mins). Pour in soy sauce, and stir to evenly coat all ingredients (1-2 mins). Serve hot. Enjoy your meal!

2. Snap Pea Jasmine Rice Stir-Fry

(4 servings, 350 kcal/serving, Cooking time: 25 minutes, Proteins: 8g, Fats: 8g, Carbs: 64g)

Ingredients:

2 cups of cooked jasmine rice (360 g)

2 cups of snap peas (208 g)

2 tbsp. of vegetable oil (28 g)

1/4 cup of soy sauce (60 ml)

1 tbsp minced ginger (6 g)

Salt, black pepper to taste

Cooking:

Heat oil in a wok. Add snap peas, and stir-fry until tender yet still crisp (3-5 mins). Stir in cooked jasmine rice, and mix well (2-3 mins). Stir in soy sauce, coating all ingredients evenly (1-2 mins). Serve immediately. Enjoy your meal!

3. Quinoa and Baby Corn Stir-Fry

(4 servings, 350 kcal/serving, Cooking time: 25 minutes, Proteins: 12g, Fats: 8g, Carbs: 58g)

Ingredients:

2 cups of cooked quinoa (408 g)

1 cup of baby corn (160 g)

1/2 cup of snow peas (72 g)

1 tbsp. of vegetable oil (28 g)

1/4 cup of soy sauce (60 ml)

1 tbsp. minced garlic (6 g)

Salt, black pepper to taste

Cooking:

Heat oil in the wok. Add baby corn and snow peas, and stir-fry until tender-crisp (4-6 mins). Stir in cooked quinoa, and mix well (2-3 mins). Pour in soy sauce, and stir to coat all ingredients evenly (1-2 mins). Serve piping hot. Enjoy your meal!

4. Wild Rice and Mushroom Medley

(4 servings, 350 kcal/serving, Cooking time: 35 minutes, Proteins: 13g, Fats: 9g, Carbs: 56g)

Ingredients:

2 cups of cooked wild rice (352 g)

0,22 lbs. mushrooms (100 g)

0,5 red bell pepper (75 g)

2 tbsp. of vegetable oil (28 g)

1/4 cup of soy sauce (60 ml)

1 tbsp. minced garlic (6 g)

Salt, black pepper to taste

Cooking:

Heat oil in the wok. Stir-fry the mushrooms and bell pepper until tender (5-7 mins). Add in the cooked wild rice, and stir well to combine (2-3 mins). Pour in the soy sauce, and mix until all ingredients are well coated (1-2 mins). Serve hot. Enjoy your meal!

5. Asparagus Barley Stir-Fry

(4 servings, 360 kcal/serving, Cooking time: 30 minutes, Proteins: 11g, Fats: 9g, Carbs: 62g)

Ingredients:

1 cup of cooked barley (396 g)

134 g of asparagus

2 tbsp. of vegetable oil (28 g)

1/4 cup of soy sauce (60 ml)

1 tbsp. minced garlic (6 g)

Salt, black pepper to taste

Cooking:

Heat oil in the wok.

Add asparagus, and stir-fry until tender (4-6 mins). Stir in cooked barley, and mix well (2-3 mins). Add soy sauce, and stir until all ingredients are evenly coated (1-2 mins).

Serve immediately. Enjoy your meal!

6. Snow Pea Millet Stir-Fry

(4 servings, 340 kcal/serving, Cooking time: 30 minutes, Proteins: 11g, Fats: 8g, Carbs: 60g)

Ingredients:

2 cups of cooked millet (378 g)

1 cup of snow peas (116 g)

1 red bell pepper (100 g)

1 tbsp. of vegetable oil (28 g)

1/4 cup of soy sauce (60 ml)

1 tbsp minced garlic (6 g)

Salt, black pepper to taste

Cooking:

Heat oil in the wok. Stir-fry snow peas and bell pepper until crisp-tender (4-6 mins). Stir in the cooked millet, and combine well (2-3 mins). Pour in soy sauce, coat all ingredients (1-2 mins). Serve hot. Enjoy your meal!

---

7. Veggie Udon Noodle Wok

(4 servings, 340 kcal/serving, Cooking Time: 30 minutes, Proteins: 9g, Fats: 10g, Carbohydrates: 55g)

Ingredients:

200 g udon noodles

0,5 red bell pepper (60 g)

1 carrot (150 g)

2 tbsp. soy sauce (30 ml)

1 tbsp. sesame oil (15 ml)

2 cloves of garlic, minced (about 6 g)

2 tbsp. vegetable oil (30 ml)

Salt, pepper - to taste

Cooking:

Cook the noodles as per the directions provided on the packaging.

Cut the carrot into strips while the noodles cook and the bell pepper into slices. Finely chop the garlic. In a heated wok, fry the garlic in oil until golden. Add the carrot and pepper, and fry for about 5 minutes. Add the boiled noodles, soy, and sesame sauce. Stir well and fry for a couple more minutes.

Serve hot. Enjoy your meal!

8. Sweet and Sour Noodle Wok

(4 servings, 360 kcal/serving, Cooking Time: 35 minutes, Proteins: 10g, Fats: 10g, Carbohydrates: 58g)

Ingredients:

200 g of noodles (any type)

2 carrots (280 g)

2 tomatoes (340 g)

4 tbsp. of sweet and sour sauce (60 ml)

2 tbsp. of vegetable oil (30 ml)

2 cloves of garlic, minced (6 g)

Salt, pepper - to taste

Cooking:

Cook the noodles as per the directions provided on the packaging and set aside. Cut the carrots into strips and the tomatoes into cubes. Mince the garlic. In a hot wok, fry the garlic in vegetable oil until golden. Add the carrots and tomatoes, and fry, stirring, for about 5 minutes.

Add the sweet and sour sauce, mix it well, and continue to sauté for a few more minutes. Add the noodles to the wok, mix all the ingredients well, and cook for another 2-3 minutes. Delicious to serve hot. Enjoy your meal!

9. Broccoli Quinoa Stir-Fry

(4 servings, 310 kcal/serving, Cooking time: 25 minutes, Proteins: 13g, Fats: 8g, Carbs: 47g)

Ingredients:

2 cups of cooked quinoa (374 g)

1/2 of broccoli (100 g)

2 tbsp. of vegetable oil (30 ml)

1/4 cup of soy sauce (60 ml)

1 tbsp. minced garlic (6 g)

Salt, pepper - to taste

Cooking:

Heat oil in the wok.

Add broccoli, and stir-fry until tender (4-6 mins). Add cooked quinoa, and blend well with the broccoli (2-3 mins). Pour in soy sauce, and stir until all ingredients are evenly coated (1-2 mins). Serve hot. Enjoy your meal!

10. Chicken and Zucchini Noodle Wok

(4 servings, 550 kcal/serving, Cooking Time: 35 minutes, Proteins: 30g, Fats: 15g, Carbohydrates: 70g)

Ingredients:

0,88 lbs. of chicken breast (400 g)

3 cups of noodles (300 g)

2 zucchinis (600 g)

2 tbsp. of soy sauce (30 ml)

2 tbsp. of vegetable oil (30 ml)

2 cloves of garlic (6 g),

Salt, pepper - to taste

Cooking:

Cut the chicken breast and fry in hot oil in a wok. Add minced garlic, and quickly fry. Add chopped zucchini, fry for a couple of minutes. Boil the noodles separately until half-cooked, then drain. Incorporate the noodles into the wok, followed by soy sauce, salt, and pepper, mix everything thoroughly, and proceed to sauté for an additional 5 minutes. Serve hot. Enjoy your meal!

11. Tiger Shrimp Udon Noodle Wok

(4 servings, 580 kcal/serving, Cooking Time: 40 minutes, Proteins: 24g, Fats: 14g, Carbohydrates: 90g)

Ingredients:

1 cup of udon noodles (400 g)

0,65 lbs. of tiger shrimp (600 g)

2 tbsp. of vegetable oil (30 ml)

2 tbsp. of soy sauce (30 ml)

1.5 cups of green beans (200 g)

2 cloves of garlic, minced (6 g)

Salt, pepper - to taste

Cooking:

Warm up the wok and introduce the vegetable oil. Add the peeled shrimp and fry until they turn pink (2-4 mins). Add minced garlic and green beans, and continue frying (3-5 mins). Add boiled udon noodles to the wok, then soy sauce, salt, and pepper mix well (2-3 mins). Fry everything together for a few more minutes (2-3 mins). Serve hot. Enjoy your meal!

12. Meatball Noodle Wok

(4 servings, 550 kcal/serving, Cooking Time: 45 minutes, Proteins: 30g, Fats: 25g, Carbohydrates: 50g)

Ingredients:

1,1 lbs. of ground meat (500 g)

3 cups of noodles (300 g)

1 onion (225 g)

2 tbsp. of soy sauce (30 ml)

2 tbsp. of oil (30 ml)

Salt, pepper - to taste

Cooking:

Form and season meatballs from ground meat (10 mins). In a wok, fry meatballs until cooked (5 mins). Add chopped onion, fry until golden (5 mins). Separately, cook noodles as per package instructions (usually 10 mins). Mix well with noodles and soy sauce to WOK (2 mins). Fry to blend flavors (2 mins). Serve hot. Enjoy your meal!

13. Teriyaki Udon Noodle Wok

(4 servings, 570 kcal/serving, Cooking time: 35 minutes, Proteins: 18g, Fats: 15g, Carbohydrates: 92g)

Ingredients:

5 cups of udon noodles (500 g)

1/2 cup of teriyaki sauce (120 ml)

1/2 cup of vegetable broth (120 ml)

1 red pepper sliced (120 g)

1 head of broccoli (200 g)

1 carrot (80 g)

2 tbsp. of oil (vegetable or a mix of olive and sesame) (30 ml)

Salt, black pepper - to taste

Cooking:

Boil Udon noodles, drain, and set aside (8-10 mins). Sauté carrot, broccoli, and red pepper in WOK until slightly soft (5-7 mins). Mix in noodles and teriyaki sauce until evenly coated (2-3 mins). Add vegetable broth, and let noodles absorb flavors (2-3 mins). Serve hot. Enjoy your meal!

---

14. Sweet and Sour Pork Rice Noodle Wok

(4 servings, 600 kcal/serving, Cooking Time: 40 minutes, Proteins: 35g, Fats: 15g, Carbohydrates: 70g)

Ingredients:

1,1 lbs. of pork (500 g)

2 cups of rice noodles (200 g)

1 red pepper (120 g)

1 carrot (80 g)

4 tbsp. of sweet and sour sauce (60 ml)

2 cloves of garlic, minced (10 g)

2 tbsp. of soybean oil (30 ml)

Salt, black pepper - to taste

Cooking:

Slice pork into thin strips. Heat the oil in the WOK over a medium flame and brown the pork, which should take approximately 5-7 minutes. Add carrot, red pepper, and garlic, and sauté until veggies are soft (5-7 mins). Add sweet and sour sauce, and toss to coat meat and veggies (2 mins). Cook rice noodles as per packet instructions, add to WOK, and throw everything together (5-10 mins). Serve hot. Enjoy your meal!

15. Pork, Beans and Ginger Noodle Wok

(4 servings, 600 kcal/serving, Cooking Time: 40 minutes, Proteins: 35g, Fats: 25g, Carbohydrates: 55g)

Ingredients:

0,88 lbs. of pork (400 g)

2 cups of noodles (200 g)

1 1/2 cups of green beans (200 g)

1 piece of ginger (15 g),

2 cloves of garlic (10 g)

3 tbsp. of soy sauce (45 ml)

2 tbsp. of soybean oil (30 ml)

Salt, black pepper - to taste

Cooking:

Cut the pork into small pieces. Heat oil in WOK over medium heat, and sauté pork until golden (5-7 mins). Add green beans, ginger, and garlic, and sauté until the beans are soft (5-7 mins). Add soy sauce, and toss to coat (2 mins). Cook noodles as instructed, add to WOK, and toss together (5-10 mins). Serve hot. Enjoy your meal!

Chapter 8: Soups and Broths

1. Chicken Tom Yam
(4 servings, 200 kcal/serving, Cooking Time: 45 minutes, Proteins: 20g, Fats: 8g, Carbohydrates: 15g)

Ingredients:

0,65 lbs. of chicken fillet (300 g)

0,44 lbs. of shrimp (200 g)

0,33 lbs. mushrooms (150 g)

1 stalk of lemongrass (15 g),

2 kaffir lime leaves

1 red onion, (113 g)

3 cloves of garlic (15 g)

2 tomatoes (226 g)

1 can of coconut milk (400 ml)

3 tbsp of fish sauce (45 ml)

1 tsp of sugar (4 g)

Juice of 2 limes (60 ml)

Red chili pepper, to taste

Coriander, for serving

4.2 cups of water (1 l)

Cooking:

Chop vegetables: onion (half rings), tomatoes (cubes), garlic, chili pepper (finely), slice mushrooms, crush lemongrass (5-10 mins). Heat oil in a wok, sauté garlic, onion, lemongrass, kaffir lime leaves, and chili until onion is transparent (5 mins). Add small pieces of chicken and mushrooms, and sauté until cooked (10 mins). Add shrimp and tomatoes, and cook further (2 mins). Add coconut milk, water, fish sauce, sugar, lime juice, stir, and boil it. Simmer the soup for 10-15 mins. Serve hot, garnished with coriander. Enjoy your meal!

2. Classik Miso Soup

(4 servings, 250 kcal/serving, Cooking Time: 40 minutes, Proteins: 12g, Fats: 10g, Carbohydrates: 30g)

<u>Ingredients</u>:

3 tbsp. of miso paste (45 g)

7 oz. of tofu (200 g)

1 cup of wakame seaweed, rehydrated (10 g)

2 stalks of green onions thinly sliced (60 g),

20 g of shiitake (about 1/2 cup when rehydrated and sliced)

6.3 cups of broth (fish or vegetable) (1.5 l)

Salt, to taste

<u>Cooking</u>:

Soak wakame and shiitake in warm water (20 mins). Cut tofu into cubes and green onions into rings. Boil broth in a wok (5-10 mins). Dissolve miso paste in some broth, and add to WOK (5 mins). Add wakame, shiitake, and tofu. Let simmer (5 mins). Remove from heat. Serve hot, sprinkled with green onions. Serve the miso soup hot, sprinkled with green onions. Enjoy your meal!

3. Rice Noodle Soup with Lamb

(4 servings, 450 kcal/serving, Cooking Time: 45 minutes, Proteins: 32g, Fats: 20g, Carbohydrates: 40g)

Ingredients:

1,1 lbs. of lamb (500 g)

1 cup of rice noodles (200 g)

2 carrots (200 g)

1 leek (200 g)

4 cloves of garlic, minced (20 g)

2 tbsp of soy sauce (30 ml)

6.3 cups of water (1.5 l)

Salt and black pepper, to taste

Cooking:

Cut the meat into small pieces and fry in the wok until golden over medium heat. Cut the carrots into straws, finely chop the leek and garlic. Introduce the vegetables to the meat in the pan and proceed with the frying process for another 5-7 minutes. Then add water, soy sauce, salt, and pepper to the wok, boil, and reduce heat to low. Add the rice noodles and simmer the soup for another 10 minutes until the noodles are ready.

Serve the finished soup hot. Enjoy your meal!

---

4. Chicken and Green Pea Soup

(4 servings, 400 kcal/serving, Cooking Time: 35 minutes, Proteins: 26g, Fats: 12g, Carbohydrates: 50g)

Ingredients:

0,88 lbs of chicken fillet (400 g)

1 cup of green peas (150 g)

1 onion (150 g)

3 cloves of garlic, minced (15 g)

1 tbsp. of soy sauce (15 ml)

6.3 cups of water (1.5 l)

Salt and black pepper, to taste

Cooking:

Cut the chicken fillet into small pieces and fry in a wok until cooked about 10 minutes.

Introduce finely minced onion and garlic to the pan and sauté until they reach a golden color. Add green peas, soy sauce, salt, and pepper. Stir well and stew for 5 minutes. Pour in water, bring to a boil and simmer over low heat for about 15 minutes. The soup is ready. Serve hot. Enjoy your meal!

5. Shrimp Soup with Coconut Milk and Lemongrass
(4 servings, 350 kcal/serving, Cooking Time: 30 minutes, Proteins: 24g, Fats: 12g, Carbohydrates: 38g)

Ingredients:

0,88 lbs. of shrimp (400 g)

1 can of coconut milk (400 ml)

2 stalks of lemongrass

1 lime, juiced (30 ml of juice)

1 chili pepper (2 tsp)

1/4 cup of coriander (15 g)

4,2 cups of water (1 l)

Salt, to taste

Cooking:

In a pot filled with water, add lemongrass. Bring the mixture to a boil, then lower the heat and let it simmer for 10 minutes. Add shrimp and cook for another 5 minutes until they turn pink and begin to float. Add coconut milk and chili, and cook for another 5 minutes. Add the juice of one lime and sprigs of coriander. Your soup is ready! Serve hot, and enjoy your meal!

6. Turmeric Chicken Soup with Coconut Milk

(4 servings, 380 kcal/serving, Cooking Time: 40 minutes, Proteins: 28g, Fats: 15g, Carbohydrates: 30g)

Ingredients:

0,66 lbs. of chicken fillet (300 g)

1 can of coconut milk (400 ml)

1 tsp. of turmeric (2 g)

4.2 cups of vegetable broth (1 l)

Juice of 1/2 lemon (15 ml)

2 shallots (40 g)

Salt and black pepper, to taste

Greens for serving (15 g)

Cooking:

Cut the chicken fillet into small pieces. On medium heat in a WOK, fry the chicken until golden. Add finely chopped shallots and fry until the onions become soft. Add turmeric and stir. Add vegetable broth, coconut milk, lemon juice, salt, and pepper. Simmer for 15-20 minutes. Serve hot, sprinkling with greens. Enjoy your meal!

7. Tiger Shrimp and Veggie with Udon Noodle Soup

(4 servings, 450 kcal/serving, Cooking Time: 50 minutes, Proteins: 24g, Fats: 12g, Carbohydrates: 60g)

Ingredients:

3 cups of Udon noodles (300 g)

0,44 lbs. of tiger shrimps (200 g)

6.3 cups of vegetable broth (1.5 l)

1 carrot (130 g)

1 bell pepper (150 g)

2 tbsp. of soy sauce (30 ml)

Green onion for serving (25 g)

Salt and pepper, to taste

Cooking:

Prepare Udon noodles according to the instructions on the package. While the noodles are being prepared, peel the shrimps and put them in the WOK. Introduce the vegetable broth into the mixture, let it reach a boil, and then continue to cook for 5 more minutes. Add sliced bell pepper and grated carrot, and cook for another 5 minutes. Introduce soy sauce, salt, and pepper according to your preference. Add the boiled noodles and stir. Serve hot, sprinkled with green onions. Enjoy your meal!

8. Coconut Chicken Soup with Lemongrass

(4 servings, 380 kcal/serving, Cooking Time: 45 minutes, Proteins: 30g, Fats: 10g, Carbohydrates: 40g)

Ingredients:

0,88 lbs of chicken fillet (400 g)

1 can of coconut milk (400 ml)

1 stalk of lemongrass (45 g)

6,3 cups of broth (chicken or vegetable) (1.5 l)

30 g ginger root

1 lime (30 ml when juiced)

1 red pepper (150 g)

Salt and pepper, to taste

Cooking:

Cut the chicken fillet into small pieces and put it in a preheated WOK. Add thinly sliced lemongrass and ginger, and fry with the chicken for 5 minutes. Pour in the broth and simmer for another 10 minutes. Add coconut milk, chopped red pepper, and lime juice, and cook for another 5-7 minutes. Salt and pepper to taste. Serve the soup hot, garnished with fresh coriander leaves. Enjoy your meal!

9. Tiger Prawn Laksa Soup

(4 servings, 400 kcal/serving, Cooking Time: 45 minutes, Proteins: 20g, Fats: 15g, Carbohydrates: 50g)

Ingredients:

0,88 lbs. of tiger prawns (400 g)

2.5 cups of vermicelli (200 g)

1 can of coconut milk (400 ml)

4.2 cups of broth (chicken or fish) (1 l)

30 g ginger root

2 shallots (120 g)

3 cloves of garlic minced (9 g)

2 tbsp. of soy sauce (30 ml)

1 red pepper (150 g)

A small bunch of cilantro (15 g)

Salt and pepper, to taste

Cooking:

Shell the prawns, leaving a few wholes for decoration. Don't throw away the heads and shells - we'll make a broth from them. Finely chop the shallots, garlic, and ginger. Fry them in a WOK together with the prawn heads and shells. Introduce the broth and allow it to simmer for a duration of 10 minutes. Then strain the broth and return it to the WOK. Add the coconut milk, soy sauce, chopped red pepper, and cilantro, and simmer for 5 minutes. Add the vermicelli and shelled prawns, and cook until the vermicelli is ready. Salt and pepper to taste. Serve the soup hot, decorated with whole prawns and a sprig of cilantro. Enjoy your meal!

10. Tofu Soup with Shiitake Mushrooms

(4 servings, 350 kcal/serving, Cooking Time: 35 minutes, Proteins: 12g, Fats: 14g, Carbohydrates: 45g)

Ingredients:

7 oz. of tofu (200 g)

0,33 lbs. of shiitake mushrooms (150 g)

1 bunch of green onions (150 g)

4.2 cups of chicken broth (1 l)

20 g ginger root

2 tbsp. of soy sauce (30 ml)

Salt and pepper, to taste

Cooking:

Cut the tofu into cubes. If the shiitake mushrooms are dried, soak them in warm water beforehand. Slice the ginger into thin pieces. In a WOK, heat up the broth, add the ginger, and simmer for 5 minutes. Incorporate the mushrooms and tofu into the mix and allow it to simmer for another 10 minutes. Afterward, add soy sauce, salt, and pepper according to your preference. Serve the soup hot, garnished with sliced green onions. Enjoy your meal!

---

11. Shrimp Tom Yam

(4 servings, 250 kcal/serving, Cooking Time: 35 minutes, Proteins: 16g, Fats: 10g, Carbohydrates: 20g)

Ingredients:

0,66 lbs. of shrimps (300 g)

0,22 lbs. of mushrooms (200 g)

1 stem of lemongrass

3 Kaffir lime leaves

1 piece of Galangal root (can be replaced with ginger) (25 g)

100 g of cherry tomatoes

2 shallots (60 g)

2 tbsp. of lemon juice (30 ml)

2 tbsp. of fish sauce (30 ml)

1 red chili pepper (10 g)

Coriander, to taste

Salt, to taste

Cooking:

Peel the shrimps but leave the tails on. Slice the mushrooms thinly. Finely chop the lemongrass, kaffir lime leaves, and galangal (or ginger). In a WOK, pour 1 liter of water, add lemongrass, kaffir lime leaves, and galangal and cook for 10 minutes. Add the mushrooms, shrimps, sliced shallots, and cherry tomatoes. Cook for another 5-7 minutes. In the end, add lemon juice, fish sauce, sliced chili pepper, and salt to taste. Serve the soup hot, sprinkled with chopped coriander. Enjoy your meal!

12. Thai Chicken and Coconut Milk Soup

(4 servings, 430 kcal/serving, Cooking Time: 35 minutes, Proteins: 30g, Fats: 25g, Carbohydrates: 20g)

Ingredients:

1,1 lbs. of chicken fillet (500 g)

1 can of coconut milk (400 ml)

4,2 cups of chicken broth (1 L)

0,44 lbs. of shiitake mushrooms (200 g)

2 stems of lemongrass

2 limes (125 g)

Coriander - to taste

Salt, black pepper - to taste

Cooking:

Cut the chicken fillet into small pieces. Clean and slice the mushrooms. In a WOK, heat the coconut milk over medium heat until the first bubbles appear, add the chicken fillet and mushrooms. Chop the lemongrass, and add it to the WOK. Simmer for about 15 minutes. Introduce the broth to the mixture, and adjust the flavor with salt and pepper according to your preference. Cook for another 10 minutes. Prior to serving, squeeze the juice of two limes into the soup and garnish it with finely chopped coriander. Serve hot. Enjoy your meal!

---

13. Seafood Medley Soup

(4 servings, 300 kcal/serving, Cooking Time: 40 minutes, Proteins: 25g, Fats: 8g, Carbohydrates: 35g)

Ingredients:

0,44 lbs. of shrimps (200 g)

0,44 lbs. of mussels (200 g)

0,44 lbs. of squids (200 g)

 4.2 cups of vegetable broth (1 L)

1 carrot (80 g)

1 bell pepper (149 g)

1 onion (180 g)

2 cloves of garlic (6 g)

2 tbsp. of soy sauce (30 ml)

1 tbsp. of lemon juice (15 ml)

Greens (dill, parsley) - to taste

Salt, pepper - to taste

Cooking:

Rinse and clean the shrimps, mussels, and squids. Cut the carrot, pepper, and onion into julienne strips, chop the garlic. In a WOK, heat a little oil, fry the vegetables until golden, add garlic, and fry for another couple of minutes. Add the seafood to the WOK, and fry everything together for about 5 minutes. Pour the broth into the WOK, bring it to a boil, and simmer for about 10 minutes. Finish cooking by adding soy sauce, lemon juice, salt, and pepper to taste. Stir. Serve the soup hot, sprinkled with fresh herbs. Enjoy your meal!

14. Red Onion and Pumpkin Soup

(4 servings, 250 kcal/serving, Cooking Time: 45 minutes,Proteins: 6g, Fats: 10g, Carbohydrates: 30g)

Ingredients:

2 red onions (300 g)

1,1 lbs. of pumpkin (500 g)

6,3 cups of vegetable broth (1.5 L)

1/3 cup of red wine (100 ml)

1 tsp. of sugar (4 g)

3 tbsp. of cream (50 ml)

1 tsp. of thyme

Salt, black pepper - to taste

Cooking:

Peel the pumpkin, and cut it into cubes. Chop the onion. In a WOK, heat a little oil, fry the onion with sugar until golden. Add the pumpkin to the WOK, and fry for another 5 minutes. Pour wine into the WOK, and give it a couple of minutes to partially evaporate. Subsequently, add the broth to your cooking pot, increase the heat until the mixture begins to boil, then decrease the heat and allow the pumpkin to simmer until it reaches a tender consistency, which should typically take around 30 minutes. Once done, use a blender to process the soup until it attains a smooth consistency. Add cream, thyme, salt, and pepper to taste, and stir.

Serve the soup hot. Enjoy your meal!

15. Mussel Soup with Lemongrass

(4 servings, 320 kcal/serving, Cooking Time: 45 minutes, Proteins: 25g, Fats: 10g, Carbohydrates: 25g)

Ingredients:

1,1 lbs of mussels (500 g)
4,2 cups of fish broth (1 l)
2 stems of lemongrass
1 lemon (60 g)
2 cloves of garlic (6 g)
Parsley - to taste
Salt, black pepper - to taste

Cooking:

Rinse the mussels thoroughly. In a sizable pot, bring the broth to a boiling point. Introduce the mussels to the pot and let them cook over a medium flame for roughly 5 minutes or until you notice the shells opening. Chop the lemongrass and garlic. Slice the lemon into thin slices. In a WOK, warm the oil and sauté the garlic until it achieves a golden hue.

Add the lemongrass and lemon slices, and fry for another minute. Transfer the mussels along with the broth to the WOK, and bring to a boil. Cook for another 5 minutes. The soup is ready. Season with salt and pepper as per your liking, and stir in finely chopped parsley.

 Serve hot. Enjoy your meal!

Chapter 9: Salads

1. Shrimp Avocado Salad

(4 servings, 360 kcal/serving, Cooking Time: 20 minutes, Proteins: 20g, Fats: 22g, Carbohydrates: 20g)

Ingredients:

2 avocados (400 g)

0,88 lbs. of shrimp (400 g)

1 lemon (100 g)

2 cloves of garlic (6 g)

2 tbsp of olive oil (30 ml)

Salt, black pepper - to taste

Greens for decoration (amount varies based on preference)

Cooking:

Sauté garlic-sliced shrimp in olive oil in a WOK until golden (5 mins). Dice peeled avocado. Combine with shrimp in a salad bowl. Season with lemon juice, salt, and pepper. Toss and garnish with greens. Enjoy!

2. Chicken Mango Salad

(4 servings, 310 kcal/serving, Cooking Time: 25 minutes, Proteins: 22g, Fats: 14g, Carbohydrates: 22g)

Ingredients:

0,66 lbs. of chicken breast (300 g)

1 mango (213 g)

1 red onion (128 g)

2 tbsp of soy sauce (30 ml)

1 lime (100 g)

1 tbsp of vegetable oil (15 ml)

Salt, pepper - to taste

Cooking:

Slice chicken into thin strips and sear in a hot WOK until cooked, then set aside (5 mins). Peel and slice mango, finely chop onion. In the same WOK, sauté mango and onion briefly (2 mins). Add soy sauce, lime juice, stir, and heat briefly (1 min). Add chicken back, season, and stir well. Enjoy!

3.Tuna Avocado Mix

(4 servings, 350 kcal/serving, Cooking Time: 20 minutes, Proteins: 28g, Fats: 20g, Carbohydrates: 12g)

Ingredients:

0,88 lbs. of tuna (400 g)

2 avocados (200 g)

200 g of cherry tomatoes

2 tbsp. of soy sauce (30 ml)

1 lime (100 g)

1 tbsp. of vegetable oil (15 ml)

Salt, pepper - to taste

Cooking:

Cut tuna into pieces and quick-fry in WOK with oil until cooked, then transfer to a plate (5 mins). Peel and chop avocado, and cut cherry tomatoes in half. In the same WOK, fry avocado and tomatoes briefly (2 mins). Add soy sauce, lime juice, stir, and heat together (1 min). Add tuna back, season, and stir well. Enjoy your meal!

4. Mango Chicken Salad

(4 servings, 320 kcal/serving, Cooking Time: 30 minutes, Proteins: 30g, Fats: 12g, Carbohydrates: 20g)

Ingredients:

1,06 lbs. of chicken breast (500 g)

1 mango (400 g)

0,44 lbs. of lettuce leaves (200 g)

2 tbsp. of soy sauce (30 ml)

1 tbsp. of honey (15 ml)

1 tbsp. of vegetable oil (15 ml)

Salt, pepper - to taste

Cooking:

Fry chicken strips in WOK with oil until cooked. Season and mix with soy sauce and honey (10 mins). Peel and cube mango (5 mins). Tear lettuce into pieces. Combine chicken, mango, and lettuce in WOK. Heat briefly (2 mins). Enjoy!

5. Warm Shrimp Avocado Medley

(4 servings, 260 kcal/serving, Cooking Time: 25 minutes, Proteins: 20g, Fats: 15g, Carbohydrates: 12g)

Ingredients:

1.1 lbs. of shrimps (500 g)

2 avocados (200 g)

200 g of cherry tomatoes

1 lemon (113 g)

2 tbsp. of olive oil (30 ml)

Salt and pepper - to taste

Cooking:

In a WOK, fry shrimps in olive oil until pink (5 mins). Cube an avocado, halve cherry tomatoes. Add to WOK. Season with lemon juice, salt, and pepper. Mix and heat for 2 mins. Enjoy!

6. Chicken and Mangosteen Salad

(4 servings, 240 kcal/serving, Cooking Time: 35 minutes, Proteins: 25g, Fats: 9g, Carbohydrates: 15g)

Ingredients:

0,88 lbs. of chicken fillet (400 g)

2 mangosteens (150 g)

1 carrot (70 g)

2 stalks of celery (80 g)

1 lemon (113 g)

2 tbsp of soy sauce (30 ml)

Salt and pepper - to taste

Cooking:

In a WOK, fry small chicken pieces until done (10 mins). Extract pulp from halved mangosteen. Julienne carrots and celery. Add everything to the WOK with soy sauce, lemon juice, salt, and pepper. Stir and cook for 2 mins. Enjoy your warm chicken and mangosteen salad! The chicken and mangosteen salad is ready to be served! Enjoy your meal!

7. Tiger Shrimp and Avocado Salad in WOK

(4 servings, 350 kcal/serving, Cooking Time: 30 minutes, Proteins: 25g, Fats: 15g, Carbohydrates: 10g)

Ingredients:

0.88 lbs. tiger shrimp (400 g)

2 avocados - (250 g)

200 g cherry tomatoes

1 lime (100 g)

2 tbsp. olive oil (30 g)

Salt and pepper - to taste

Cooking:

Sauté shrimp in a WOK with olive oil until golden (5 mins). Add cubed avocado, halved cherry tomatoes, lime juice, salt, and pepper. Stir and cook together for 2 more mins. Enjoy!

8. Shrimp and Mango Eastern Salad

(4 servings, 310 kcal/serving, Cooking Time: 30 minutes, Proteins: 16g, Fats: 8g, Carbohydrates: 40g)

Ingredients:

0,66 lbs. shrimp (300 g)

2 mangoes (500 g)

2 cucumbers (200 g)

1 red onion (100 g)

1 bunch of coriander (25 g)

1 lime (100 g)

2 tbsp. soy sauce (15 g)

Salt, pepper - to taste

Cooking:

In a WOK, sauté shrimp until golden, about 4 minutes. Add thin strips of mango and cucumber, onion rings, lime juice, soy sauce, salt, and pepper. Cook, stirring occasionally, for about 6 minutes. Top with coriander and serve. Enjoy!

---

9. Chicken, Avocado, and Pepper Salad

(4 servings, 470 kcal/serving, Cooking Time: 35 minutes, Proteins: 28g, Fats: 28g, Carbohydrates: 22g)

Ingredients:

1,1 lbs. chicken breast (500 g)

2 avocados (250 g)

1 red pepper (200 g)

1 bunch of romaine lettuce (225 g)

1 Lemon (113 g)

2 tbsp olive oil (14 g)

Salt, pepper - to taste

Cooking:

In a WOK, fry the chicken breast until done, about 7-8 minutes. Remove it from the WOK, let it cool, and cut into strips. Dice the avocado and red pepper, and cut the romaine lettuce into strips. Add the chicken strips, diced avocado, red pepper, and lettuce in the same WOK. Squeeze the juice of a lemon, add olive oil, salt, and pepper to taste. Stir everything and heat over medium heat for about 5-7 minutes. Serve the salad warm. Enjoy your meal!

10. Thai Shrimp and Mango Salad

(4 servings, 350 kcal/serving, Cooking Time: 30 minutes, Proteins: 22g, Fats: 12g, Carbohydrates: 40g)

Ingredients:

0,88 lbs. shrimp (400 g)

2 mangoes (800 g)

1 red onion (150 g)

1 bunch of cilantro (100 g)

1 lime (100 g)

1 red chili (10 g)

2 tbsp. olive oil (14 g)

Salt - to taste

Cooking:

In a WOK, fry the shrimp until they turn pink, about 4-5 minutes. Set them aside. Slice the mango and red onion into thin strips. Return the shrimp to the WOK. Add the sliced mango and onion, grated lime zest and juice, finely chopped chili, and cilantro. Finish off the dish by drizzling some olive oil over it and seasoning with salt as per your taste preference. Stir all the ingredients and heat over medium heat for about 4-5 minutes. Enjoy your meal!

11. Beef and Sesame Salad

(4 servings, 390 kcal/serving, Cooking Time: 30 minutes, Proteins: 24g, Fats: 18g, Carbohydrates: 33g)

Ingredients:

0,88 lbs. beef (400 g)

2 carrots (200 g)

2 bell peppers (200 g)

0,11 lbs. sesame seeds (50 g)

3 tbsp. of soy sauce (50 ml)

2 tbsp. Vegetable oil (50 ml)

Salt, pepper - to taste

Cooking:

Slice the beef into thin strips and fry in a WOK in vegetable oil until done. Salt and pepper to taste. Slice the carrots and bell peppers into strips and add to the WOK with the beef. Fry for another 5 minutes. Pour all with soy sauce and sprinkle with sesame seeds. Stir everything and cook for another 2-3 minutes. Serve the salad warm. Enjoy your meal!

12. Veggie Shrimp Salad

(4 servings, 320 kcal/serving, Cooking Time: 25 minutes, Proteins: 30g, Fats: 8g, Carbohydrates: 32g)

Ingredients:

1,1 lbs. shrimps (500 g)
1 small head of broccoli (200 g)
2 carrots (200 g)
2 cucumbers (300 g)
3 tbsp soy sauce (50 ml)
2 tbsp olive oil (14 g)
Salt, pepper - to taste

Cooking:

Fry the shrimps in olive oil in a WOK until they turn pink, salt and pepper to taste. Then place them on a plate. In the same WOK, fry the broccoli and the julienned carrots for about 5-7 minutes. Cut the cucumbers into strips and add them to the WOK. Fry everything together for another 2-3 minutes. Return the shrimps to the WOK, pour all with soy sauce, mix well, and cook for a couple more minutes.
Serve the salad warm. Enjoy your meal!

13. Tuna and Bell Pepper Salad

(4 servings, 350 kcal/serving, Cooking Time: 20 minutes, Proteins: 45g, Fats: 6g, Carbohydrates: 25g)

Ingredients

1,1 lbs. Fresh Tuna (500 g)
1 red bell pepper (200 g)
1 head iceberg lettuce (200 g)
2 garlic cloves (10 g)
3 tbsp. of soy sauce (50 ml)
2 tbsp. olive oil (14 g)
Salt, black pepper - to taste

Cooking:

Cut the tuna into small pieces, salt, pepper, and fry in olive oil in a WOK until done. Then place it on a plate. In the same WOK, fry the julienned red bell pepper and minced garlic for about 5-7 minutes. Add the chopped iceberg lettuce, tuna, pour in soy sauce and mix everything together, frying for a couple more minutes. Serve the salad warm. Enjoy your meal!

14. Avocado Chicken Salad

(4 servings, 350 kcal/serving, Cooking Time: 20 minutes, Proteins: 25g, Fats: 20g, Carbohydrates: 15g)

Ingredients:

0,66 lbs. Chicken fillet (300 g)
2 Avocados (250 g)
200 g Cherry tomatoes
1 Lime (100 g)
3 tbsp of soy sauce (50 ml)
2 tbsp Olive oil (30 ml)
Salt, black pepper - to taste

Cooking:

Cut the chicken fillet into small pieces and fry in a WOK with olive oil until golden brown.
Add the halved cherry tomatoes and continue to cook for another 5 minutes. While the chicken and tomatoes are cooking, dice the avocado. Put the chicken and tomatoes in a large bowl, add the avocado, soy sauce, and squeeze in the lime juice. Stir all the ingredients. The salad is ready to serve. Enjoy your meal!

15. Tuna Avocado Salad

(4 servings, 360 kcal/serving, Cooking Time: 20 minutes, Proteins: 25g, Fats: 20g, Carbohydrates: 25g)

Ingredients:

0.88 lbs. tuna (canned) (400 g)
2 avocados (250 g)
1 head of romaine lettuce (200 g)
1 Lemon (100 g)
2 tbsp Olive oil (30 ml)
Salt, black pepper - to taste

Cooking:

Open the canned tuna and drain off any excess liquid. Cut the avocado into cubes and the romaine lettuce into strips. In a separate bowl, mix the juice of one lemon, olive oil, salt, and pepper to make the dressing. This should take about 5 minutes. In the WOK, combine the tuna, avocado, and lettuce. Add the prepared dressing and mix well for around 2 minutes. Enjoy!

Chapter 10: Beans and Legumes

1. Pork and White Bean Medley

(4 servings, 570 kcal/serving, Cooking Time: 40 minutes, Proteins: 32g, Fats: 22g, Carbohydrates: 48g)

Ingredients:

1,1 lbs. pork (500 g)
1 can white beans (canned) (400 g)
2 tbsp. soy sauce (30 ml)
2 tbsp. olive oil (30 ml)
4 cloves garlic (15 g)
Salt, pepper - to taste

Cooking:

Cut the pork into small pieces. Start with warming up the olive oil in your WOK. Once hot, add the pork and fry until it achieves a beautiful golden brown color. For added taste, introduce minced garlic and season with salt and pepper to your liking. Continue to cook, ensuring everything is well mixed. Continue frying for 2-3 minutes. Add the beans and soy sauce. Mix well and cook for another 5 minutes. Serve hot. Enjoy your meal!

2. Tiger Shrimp and Green Bean Stir-Fry

(4 servings, 400 kcal/serving, Cooking Time: 30 minutes, Proteins: 30g, Fats: 15g, Carbohydrates: 30g)

Ingredients:

1.1 lbs. tiger shrimps (500 g)
2 cups green beans (200 g)
2 tbsp. soy sauce (30 ml)
2 tbsp. olive oil (30 ml)
4 cloves garlic (15 g)
Salt, pepper - to taste

Cooking:

Peel the shrimps and remove the intestines. Boil the green beans in boiling water for 2 minutes. Then drain and rinse with cold water. In the WOK, first, warm up your olive oil. Once it's hot, toss in the minced garlic for a quick sauté. After that, it's time to add the shrimps to the mix. Fry for 2-3 minutes until pink. Add the beans, soy sauce, salt and pepper. Stir and cook for another 2 minutes. Serve hot. Enjoy your meal!

3. Red Bean and Tofu Mix

(4 servings, 420 kcal/serving, Cooking Time: 40 minutes, Proteins: 25g, Fats: 15g, Carbohydrates: 45g)

Ingredients:

2 cups red beans (400 g)

10,56 oz. tofu (300 g)

2 tbsp. olive oil (30 ml)

2 tbsp. soy sauce (30 ml)

3 cloves garlic minced (10 g)

Salt, pepper - to taste

Cooking:

Cut the tofu into small cubes. Warm the olive oil in the WOK. Add minced garlic, and sauté until golden. Then add tofu and fry until it's golden too.

Add the beans, soy sauce, salt and pepper. Combine all the ingredients in the WOK and let it simmer on a low flame for around 15 minutes. Serve hot. Enjoy your meal!

4. Tofu and Bean Curry

(4 servings, 550 kcal/serving, Cooking Time: 40 minutes, Proteins: 25g, Fats: 30g, Carbohydrates: 50g)

Ingredients:

2 cups beans (any type, pre-soaked or canned) (400 g)

10,56 oz. tofu (300 g)

2 tbsp. curry (20 g)

1 can coconut milk (400 ml)

1 onion chopped (113 g)

2 cloves garlic minced (5 g)

2 tbsp. oil (vegetable or olive) (30 ml)

Salt, pepper - to taste

Cooking:

Cut the tofu into small cubes.

Warm the oil in the WOK, then introduce the diced onion and sauté until it turns a golden color. Add the minced garlic and curry, and fry for another couple of minutes. Add the beans, tofu, and coconut milk. Stir and simmer for another 20 minutes. Serve hot. Enjoy your meal!

5. Pea, Mushrooms, and Veggie Stir-Fry

(4 servings, 500 kcal/serving, Cooking Time: 45 minutes, Proteins: 20g, Fats: 15g, Carbohydrates: 70g)

Ingredients:

1,5 cups peas (canned or pre-soaked) (300 g)

0,44 lbs mushrooms (any type to taste) (200 g)

2 pcs. bell peppers (400 g)

1 carrot (100 g)

1 onion (113 g)

3 cloves Garlic (5 g)

3 tbsp. Soy sauce (45 ml)

2 tbsp. Oil (vegetable or olive) (30 ml)

Salt, pepper - to taste

Cooking:

Cut the mushrooms, pepper, carrot, and onion into large pieces. In your WOK, heat the oil, then include the diced onion and carrot and sauté until they achieve a golden hue. Add the pepper, mushrooms, and peas, and mix well. Incorporate the minced garlic and soy sauce into the mix and allow it to simmer for an additional 10 minutes. Serve hot. Enjoy your meal!

6. Spinach Lentil Curry

(4 servings, 450 kcal/serving, Cooking Time: 40 minutes, Proteins: 18g, Fats: 12g, Carbohydrates: 60g)

Ingredients:

1 cup lentils (pre-soaked overnight) (200 g)
0,33 lbs. Spinach (150 g)
3 shallot onions (100 g)
1 carrot (100 g)
2 cloves garlic (5 g)
2 tbsp. curry paste (30 ml)
0,5 can coconut milk(200 ml)
2 tbsp. olive oil (30 ml)
Salt, pepper - to taste

Cooking:

Chop the shallot onions, carrot, and garlic. In a heated WOK with olive oil, fry the onions until golden. Add the carrot and fry for another 5 minutes. Add the curry paste, and stir well. Add the lentils, coconut milk, and a little water. Simmer on low heat for about 20 minutes.

When the lentils become soft, add the spinach and cook for another 5 minutes. Serve hot. Enjoy your meal!

7. WOK and Bell Pepper with Honey Sauce

(4 servings, 500 kcal/serving, Cooking Time: 30 minutes, Proteins: 25g, Fats: 10g, Carbohydrates: 75g)

Ingredients:

1 cup Soybeans (pre-soaked) (200 g)
2 bell peppers (400 g)
1 onion (100 g)
2 cloves garlic (5 g)
3 tbsp. honey (45 ml)
2 tbsp. soy sauce (30 ml)
2 tbsp. olive oil (30 ml)
Salt, pepper - to taste

Cooking:

Chop the bell pepper, onion, and garlic. In a heated WOK with olive oil, fry the onions until golden. Introduce the bell pepper to the mix and continue frying for an additional 5 minutes. Add the garlic and soybeans, and fry for another 2 minutes. In a different bowl, combine the honey with the soy sauce. Then add this mixture to the WOK. Fry everything together for another 5-7 minutes until the sauce thickens. Serve hot. Enjoy your meal!

8. Chicken and Black Bean Mix

(4 servings, 500 kcal/serving, Cooking Time: 30 minutes, Proteins: 35g, Fats: 10g, Carbohydrates: 55g)

Ingredients:

1 cup black beans (soaked overnight) (200 g)

0,44 lbs. chicken fillet (200 g)

2 medium-sized tomatoes (200 g)

2 shallots (100 g)

2 cloves garlic (5 g)

2 tbsp. olive oil (30 ml)

Salt, pepper - to taste

Cilantro - for serving

Cooking:

Cut the chicken fillet into small pieces, tomatoes into slices, and finely chop the shallots and garlic. Heat the olive oil in the WOK. Add the shallots and fry until transparent. Introduce the chicken to the mix and continue frying until it achieves a white color.

Add the tomatoes and black beans, and fry everything together for 10 minutes. Introduce garlic, salt, and pepper into the mix, combine them well, and continue frying for an additional 5 minutes.

Serve hot, sprinkling chopped cilantro on top. Enjoy your meal!

---

9. Curry with Black Beans

(4 servings, 550 kcal/serving, Cooking Time: 40 minutes, Proteins: 20g, Fats: 15g, Carbohydrates: 85g)

Ingredients:

1 cup black beans (pre-soaked overnight) (250 g)

2 carrots (200 g)

1 onion (150 g)

1 red bell pepper (150 g)

1 cup canned pineapple (200 g)

2 tsp curry powder (10 g)

2 tbsp. coconut oil (30 ml)

3 tbsp. soy sauce (45 ml)

Salt, pepper - to taste

Cilantro, mint - for serving

Cooking:

Boil the beans until ready, and drain in a colander. Cut the carrots, onions, and pepper into large slices, and cut the pineapple into cubes. Warm up the coconut oil in your WOK, then swiftly introduce the curry, stirring promptly to combine. Add the onions, carrots, and pepper, and fry until the vegetables are soft. Add the beans and pineapple, and mix. Introduce the soy sauce, then season with salt and pepper according to your preference.

Fry everything together for another 5-7 minutes. Serve hot, sprinkling fresh herbs on top. Enjoy your meal!

10. Shrimp and Green Bean Combo

(4 servings, 550 kcal/serving, Cooking Time: 30 minutes, Proteins: 25g, Fats: 15g, Carbohydrates: 75g)

Ingredients:

0,88 lbs. shrimp (400 g)

1,5 cups green beans (300 g)

1 carrot (100 g)

3 cloves garlic (15 g)

3 tbsp. soy sauce (45 ml)

1 tsp. sugar (5 g)

Salt, pepper - to taste

Sesame oil - for serving

Green onions - for serving Instructions:

Cooking:

Parboil the green beans in salted water. Drain in a colander and let rest. Cut the carrot into thin long slices, and mince the garlic.

Heat the oil in the WOK. Incorporate the garlic and carrots into the WOK, and sauté them for about 2-3 minutes. Then, add the shrimps and continue frying until they adopt a pink color.

Add the green beans, soy sauce, sugar, salt, and pepper. Fry everything together for another 5 minutes. Serve hot, sprinkling green onions on top and drops of sesame oil. Enjoy your meal!

11. Veggie Lentil Stir-Fry

(4 servings, 570 kcal/serving, Cooking Time: 35 minutes, Proteins: 18g, Fats: 20g, Carbohydrates: 85g)

Ingredients:

1 cup red lentils (200 g)

1 onion (150 g)

2 carrots (200 g)

1 bell pepper (150 g)

2 cloves garlic (6 g)

1 tsp. cumin (5 g)

1 tsp. paprika (5 g)

Salt, black pepper - to taste

2 tbsp. cooking oil (30 ml)

Herbs for serving (optional)

Cooking:

Rinse the lentils and pour cold water (1 part lentils - 2 parts water). Cook until ready, drain in a colander. Cut the carrots, onions, and bell pepper into thin strips, and chop the garlic. Heat the oil in the WOK. Add the onions and fry until they become transparent. Add the carrots and pepper, fry until they become soft. Add garlic, cumin, and paprika, and stir. Add the cooked lentils, salt, and pepper and mix well. Fry for another 5 minutes. Serve hot, sprinkling fresh herbs on top. Enjoy your meal!

12. Black Bean and Corn Mix

(4 servings, 580 kcal/serving, Cooking Time: 30 minutes, Proteins: 20g, Fats: 22g, Carbohydrates: 85g)

Ingredients:

1 cup black beans (dry or canned) (200 g)

1 can canned corn (200 g)

1 onion (150 g)

2 cloves garlic (6 g)

1 chili pepper (or to taste)

2 tbsp. olive oil (30 ml)

1 lime (about 60 g)

Salt, black pepper - to taste

Cilantro for serving

Cooking:

If you're using dry beans, soak them overnight and then boil until done. If you're using canned, simply drain and rinse. Finely chop the onion and garlic. Slice the chili pepper into rings (remove seeds if you don't want it too spicy). Warm up the oil in the WOK, and sauté the onions until they turn golden. Incorporate the garlic and chili, and continue frying for another minute. Finally, introduce the beans and corn, ensuring everything is well mixed. Fry for 5-7 minutes. Extract the juice from the lime, season with salt and pepper to taste, then stir thoroughly. Stir well. Serve with cilantro. Enjoy your meal!

13. Chickpea and Spinach Medley

(4 servings, 550 kcal/serving, Cooking Time: 35 minutes, Proteins: 25g, Fats: 18g, Carbohydrates: 80g)

Ingredients:

1 cup chickpeas (dry or canned) (200 g)

200 g fresh spinach

3 cloves garlic (15 g)

2 tbsp. olive oil (30 ml)

1/2 tsp. red pepper flakes or to taste (2,5 g)

Salt, black pepper - to taste

1 lemon (100 g)

Cooking:

If you're using dry chickpeas, soak them overnight and then boil until done. If you're using canned, simply drain and rinse. Finely chop the garlic. Heat the oil in the WOK, and fry the garlic until golden. Introduce the chickpeas to the WOK and sauté for around 5-7 minutes. Next, include the spinach and cook until it wilts, which should take roughly 3 minutes. Finally, season with red pepper flakes, salt, and black pepper according to your preference. Stir well.

Squeeze out the juice from the lemon and incorporate it into the WOK.

 Stir. Serve hot. Enjoy your meal!

14. Shrimp and Green Bean Stir-Fry

(4 servings, 500 kcal/serving, Cooking Time: 30 minutes, Proteins: 30g, Fats: 20g, Carbohydrates: 60g)

Ingredients:

1 cup green beans (400)
0,88 lbs. shrimps (400 g)
3 cloves garlic (15 g)
2 tbsp. soy sauce (30 ml)
2 tbsp. vegetable oil (30 ml)
1 tbsp. sugar (15 g)
1 lemon (100 g)
Salt, black pepper - to taste

Cooking:

Peel the shrimps if they are unpeeled. Set aside. Rinse the beans and trim the ends. Cut them into pieces about 5 cm long. Finely chop the garlic. Heat the oil in the WOK. Fry the garlic until golden. Introduce the shrimps to the pan and sauté them on medium heat until they acquire a pink color.

Add the beans and soy sauce, and sprinkle with sugar. Continue stirring while cooking over medium heat for around 5-7 minutes or until the beans soften. Season with salt and pepper to your liking, then squeeze the lemon juice into the WOK and give everything a good stir.

Serve hot. Enjoy your meal!

15. Potato and Lentil Stir-Fry

(4 servings, 550 kcal/serving, Cooking Time: 45 minutes, Proteins: 20g, Fats: 15g, Carbohydrates: 85g)

Ingredients:

1,1 lbs. potatoes (500 g)
1 cup lentils (quick cooking) (200 g)
1 onion (100 g)
1 carrot (100 g)
2 cloves garlic (10 g)
2 tsp. curry powder (10 g)
2 tbsp. olive oil (30 ml)
Salt, pepper - to taste

Cooking:

Dice the potatoes, finely slice both the carrot and onion and wash the lentils thoroughly. Warm up the oil in your WOK, and introduce the onion and carrot, frying until they soften. Following this, add in the garlic and continue to fry for a couple more minutes. Now add the potatoes, and fry them with the other ingredients for about 10 minutes.

Add lentils, curry, salt, and pepper, and pour water so that it completely covers the ingredients. Continue cooking on medium heat for roughly 20 minutes, until both the lentils and potatoes have softened.

You can sprinkle it with fresh herbs when serving. Enjoy your meal!

11. Egg and Tofu

1. Veggie Tofu Stir-Fry
(4 servings, 285 kcal/serving,
Cooking time: 20 minutes, Proteins:
21g, Fats: 11g, Carbs: 27g)
Ingredients:
14 oz. firm tofu (400 g)
2 cups mixed vegetables (300 g)
2 tbsp. vegetable oil (28 g)
1/4 cup soy sauce (60 ml)
1 tbsp. minced garlic (6 g)
1 tbsp. minced ginger (6 g)
Cooking:
Warm up the oil in the WOK using
medium heat. Add the tofu and fry
until golden. Add the vegetables,
garlic, and ginger and stir-fry until
the vegetables are tender. Stir in soy
sauce and serve hot. Enjoy your
meal!

2. Classic Egg Fried Rice
(4 servings, 315 kcal/serving, Cooking
time: 20 minutes, Proteins: 9g, Fats:
11g, Carbs: 46g)
Ingredients:
2 cups cooked rice (370 g)
2 tbsp. vegetable oil (28 g)
4 eggs, beaten (200 g)
1/2 cup frozen peas and carrots (80
g)
2 tbsp. soy sauce (30 ml)
Cooking:
Warm the oil in the WOK on a
medium heat setting. Introduce the
whisked eggs and proceed with the
cooking, ensuring you stir frequently
until the eggs are thoroughly cooked.
Introduce the peas and carrots into
the WOK, cooking them until they are
thoroughly heated. Add rice and soy
sauce and stir-fry for 3-4 minutes,
stirring constantly. Enjoy your meal!

3. Spicy Tofu with Broccoli

(4 servings, 265 kcal/serving, Cooking time: 25 minutes, Proteins: 18g, Fats: 14g, Carbs: 22g)

Ingredients:

14 oz. firm tofu (400 g)

1 head of broccoli (180 g)

2 tbsp. vegetable oil (28 g)

1/4 cup soy sauce (60 ml)

2 tbsp. sriracha sauce (30 ml)

1 tbsp. minced garlic (6 g)

Cooking:

Warm the oil in the WOK on a medium heat setting. Add the tofu and fry until golden. Add the broccoli, garlic, and stir-fry until the broccoli is tender. Stir in soy sauce and sriracha and serve hot. Enjoy your meal!

---

4. Green Onion Scramble

(4 servings, 225 kcal/serving, Cooking time: 10 minutes, Proteins: 12g, Fats: 17g, Carbs: 5g)

Ingredients:

6 eggs, beaten (300 g)

2 tbsp. vegetable oil (28 g)

1/2 cup chopped green onions (50 g)

Salt and pepper to taste

Cooking:

Warm the oil in the WOK on a medium heat setting. Add the green onions and sauté until fragrant. Add the beaten eggs, salt, and pepper. Cook, stirring constantly, until eggs are set. Serve hot. Enjoy your meal!

5. Peanut Pepper Tofu

(4 servings, 305 kcal/serving, Cooking time: 25 minutes, Proteins: 20g, Fats: 19g, Carbs: 18g)

Ingredients:

14 oz. firm tofu (400 g)

1 bell pepper (150 g)

1/4 cup unsalted peanuts (36 g)

2 tbsp. vegetable oil (28 g)

1/4 cup soy sauce (60 ml)

1 tbsp minced garlic (6 g)

Cooking:

Warm the oil in the WOK on a medium heat setting. Add the tofu and fry until golden.

Introduce the bell pepper and garlic to the WOK, stir-frying them until the pepper softens.

Stir in soy sauce and peanuts and serve hot. Enjoy your meal!

6. Egg and Tofu Stir-Fried

(4 servings, 290 kcal/serving, Cooking time: 20 minutes, Proteins: 20g, Fats: 19g, Carbs: 12g)

Ingredients:

14 oz. firm tofu (400 g)

4 large eggs, beaten (200 g)

2 tbsp. vegetable oil (28 g)

1/4 cup soy sauce (60 ml)

1 tbsp. minced garlic (6 g)

Cooking:

Warm the oil in the WOK on a medium heat setting. Add the tofu and fry until it's golden (about 5 minutes). Remove the tofu and set it aside.

In the same wok, add the beaten eggs and cook, stirring constantly, until they are set but still moist (about 3-4 minutes). Return the tofu to the wok, add the soy sauce, and stir until the ingredients are well combined (about 1-2 minutes).

Your tofu scramble is ready to serve. Serve immediately and enjoy your meal!

7. Cashew Tofu Stir-Fry

(4 servings, 320 kcal/serving, Cooking time: 20 minutes, Proteins: 17g, Fats: 22g, Carbs: 18g)

Ingredients:

14 oz. firm tofu (400 g)

1/2 cup cashews (70 g)

2 cups mixed vegetables (300 g)

2 tbsp. vegetable oil (28 g)

1/4 cup soy sauce (60 ml)

1 tbsp. minced ginger (6 g)

Cooking:

Warm the oil in the WOK on a medium heat setting. Add tofu cubes and fry until golden (around 5 minutes). Stir in your preferred veggies (such as bell pepper, broccoli, carrot, etc.) and a teaspoon of grated ginger. Cook until tender (about 5-7 minutes). Add soy sauce to taste, then add a handful of cashews, and stir well (1 minute).

Your stir-fried tofu with veggies and cashews is ready to serve. Serve hot, and enjoy your meal!

8. Green Bean Tofu Stir-Fry

(4 servings, 280 kcal/serving, Cooking time: 25 minutes, Proteins: 18g, Fats: 14g, Carbs: 25g)

Ingredients:

14 oz. firm tofu, cubed (397 g)

2 cups green beans, trimmed (250 g)

2 tbsp. vegetable oil (28 g)

1/4 cup soy sauce (60 ml)

1 tbsp. minced garlic (6 g)

Cooking:

Warm the oil in the WOK on a medium heat setting. Fry tofu until its golden (around 5 minutes). Add beans and garlic, and stir-fry until they're tender (about 5-7 minutes). Incorporate the soy sauce and continue cooking for one more minute to meld the flavors together. Your stir-fried tofu with beans and garlic is ready to serve hot. Enjoy your meal!

9. Eggplant Tofu Stir-Fry

(4 servings, 300 kcal/serving, Cooking time: 30 minutes, Proteins: 15g, Fats: 20g, Carbs: 20g)

Ingredients:

14 oz firm tofu (400 g)

1 large eggplant (550 g)

2 tbsp vegetable oil (28 g)

1/4 cup soy sauce (60 ml)

1 tbsp minced garlic (6 g)

Cooking:

Warm the oil in the WOK on a medium heat setting. Add tofu, frying until it's golden (around 5 minutes). Add eggplant and garlic to the wok, stir-frying until they're tender (about 5-7 minutes). Incorporate the soy sauce and continue cooking for one more minute to meld the flavors together. Your stir-fried tofu with eggplant is ready to serve hot. Enjoy your meal!

10. Spicy Bok Choy Tofu Stir-Fry

(4 servings, 310 kcal/serving, Cooking time: 25 minutes, Proteins: 19g, Fats: 20g, Carbs: 18g)

Ingredients:

14 oz. firm tofu (400 g)

2 cups bok choy (140 g)

2 tbsp. vegetable oil (28 g)

1/4 cup soy sauce (60 ml)

1 tbsp. minced ginger (6 g)

1 tbsp. sriracha (15 ml)

Cooking:

Warm the oil in the WOK on a medium heat setting. Add tofu, frying until it's golden (around 5 minutes).

Add bok choy and ginger to the wok, stir-frying until they're tender (about 5-7 minutes). Mix in the soy sauce and sriracha, and cook for an additional 1-2 minutes to blend the flavors. Your spicy stir-fried tofu with bok choy and ginger is ready to be served hot. Enjoy your meal!

11. Mushroom Tofu Stir-Fry
(4 servings, 320 kcal/serving, Cooking time: 30 minutes, Proteins: 21g, Fats: 20g, Carbs: 20g)
Ingredients:
14 oz. firm tofu (400 g)
2 cups mushrooms (150 g)
2 tbsp. vegetable oil (28 g)
1/4 cup soy sauce (60 ml)
1 tbsp. minced garlic (6 g)
Cooking:
Warm the oil in the WOK on a medium heat setting. Add tofu, frying until it's golden (around 5 minutes).
Add mushrooms and garlic to the wok, stir-frying until they're tender (about 5-7 minutes).
Mix in the soy sauce, cooking for an additional 1-2 minutes to combine flavors. Your stir-fried tofu with mushrooms and garlic is ready to be served hot. Enjoy your meal!

12. Sweet Sour Tofu Stir-Fry

(4 servings, 320 kcal/serving, Cooking time: 25 minutes, Proteins: 16g, Fats: 18g, Carbs: 35g)

Ingredients:

14 oz. firm tofu (400 g)

2 cups bell peppers, assorted colors (240 g)

2 tbsp. vegetable oil (28 g)

1/4 cup soy sauce (60 ml)

1 tbsp. minced garlic (6 g)

2 tbsp. honey (42 g)

2 tbsp. apple cider vinegar (30 ml)

Cooking:

Warm the oil in the WOK on a medium heat setting. Add tofu, frying until it's golden (around 5-7 minutes). Stir in bell peppers and garlic, cooking until peppers are tender (about 7-10 minutes). Add a mixture of soy sauce, honey, and vinegar, stirring for an additional 1-2 minutes to combine flavors. Serve your stir-fried tofu with bell peppers and garlic piping hot. Enjoy your meal!

13. Snow Pea Tofu Stir-Fry

(4 servings, 300 kcal/serving, Cooking time: 20 minutes, Proteins: 18g, Fats: 18g, Carbs: 20g)

Ingredients:

14 oz. firm tofu (400 g)

2 cups snow peas (160 g)

2 tbsp. vegetable oil (28 g)

1/4 cup soy sauce (60 ml)

1 tbsp. minced ginger (6 g)

Cooking:

Warm the oil in your wok over medium heat. Add the tofu, frying until it turns golden (around 5-7 minutes). Incorporate the snow peas and ginger, stir-frying until the peas are tender-crisp (about 5-6 minutes). Stir in the soy sauce, cooking for an additional 1-2 minutes to combine flavors.   Serve your stir-fried tofu with snow peas and ginger immediately. Enjoy your meal!

14. Asparagus Tofu Stir-Fry

(4 servings, 310 kcal/serving, Cooking time: 20 minutes, Proteins: 21g, Fats: 18g, Carbs: 22g)

Ingredients:

14 oz. firm tofu (400 g)

2 cups asparagus (270 g)

2 tbsp. vegetable oil (28 g)

1/4 cup soy sauce (60 ml)

1 tbsp. minced garlic (6 g)

Cooking:

Over medium heat, warm the oil in your wok. Fry the tofu in the heated oil until it's golden brown (around 5-7 minutes). Add the asparagus and garlic, stir-frying until the asparagus is tender (5-6 minutes).

Blend in the soy sauce, allowing it to cook for an additional 1-2 minutes to mix the flavors well. Serve your hot stir-fried tofu with asparagus and garlic immediately. Enjoy your meal!

15. Baby Corn Tofu Stir-Fry

(4 servings, 310 kcal/serving, Cooking time: 25 minutes, Proteins: 20g, Fats: 18g, Carbs: 25g)

Ingredients:

14 oz. firm tofu (400 g)

2 cups baby corn (256 g)

2 tbsp. vegetable oil (28 g)

1/4 cup soy sauce (60 ml)

1 tbsp. minced ginger (6 g)

Cooking:

Warm the oil in your wok over medium heat. Fry the tofu in the heated oil until it's golden brown (around 5-7 minutes). Stir in the baby corn and ginger, continuing to stir-fry until the corn is tender (5-6 minutes). Mix in the soy sauce and allow it to cook for an additional 1-2 minutes to mix the flavors well. Serve your hot stir-fried tofu with baby corn and ginger immediately. Enjoy your meal!

Chapter 12: Sauces

1. Teriyaki Magic

(4 servings, 50 kcal/serving, Cooking time: 10 minutes, Proteins: 1g, Fats: 0g, Carbs: 12g)

Ingredients:

1/4 cup sauce (60 ml)

1/4 cup mirin (60 ml)

2 tbsp. brown sugar (25 g)

Cooking:

Combine all of your chosen ingredients in your WOK. Let them simmer on medium heat for roughly 8-10 minutes until the sugar is completely dissolved and the sauce begins to thicken. After cooking, remove the wok from the heat and let your sauce cool down.

Note: Remember to stir occasionally while simmering to prevent any ingredients from sticking to the wok and ensure an evenly thickened sauce. Enjoy!

---

2. Hoisin Happiness

(4 servings, 60 kcal/serving, Cooking time: 10 minutes, Proteins: 2g, Fats: 0g, Carbs: 14g)

Ingredients:

4 tbsp. soy sauce (60 ml)

2 tbsp. peanut butter (32 g)

1 tbsp. honey (21 g)

2 tsp. rice vinegar (10 ml)

2 cloves garlic, minced (6 g)

2 tsp. sesame oil (10 ml)

Cooking:

Add all ingredients to your WOK. Over medium heat, stir continuously until all the ingredients are well combined and heated through, which should take about 8-10 minutes. Once done, remove the wok from the heat and let the sauce cool down before use. Note: Remember to stir constantly to prevent any ingredients from sticking to the wok and ensure a well-blended sauce. Enjoy your cooking!

3. Sweet and Sour Delight

(4 servings, 60 kcal/serving, Cooking time: 10 minutes, Proteins: 0g, Fats: 0g, Carbs: 15g)

Ingredients:

1/2 cup pineapple juice (120 ml)

3 tbsp. brown sugar (37 g)

3 tbsp. rice vinegar (45 ml)

2 tbsp. ketchup (34 g)

1 tbsp. cornstarch (8 g)

Cooking:

Combine all ingredients in your WOK, except for the cornstarch. Mix until well combined and heat over medium heat. Mix cornstarch with a little water to form a slurry and add to the sauce. Stir until the sauce thickens. Allow to cool before using. Enjoy your cooking!

---

4. Sizzling Szechuan

(4 servings, 70 kcal/serving, Cooking time: 10 minutes, Proteins: 1g, Fats: 3g, Carbs: 10g)

Ingredients:

1/4 cup soy sauce (60 ml)

1/4 cup water (60 ml)

2 tbsp. sriracha (30 ml)

1 tbsp. sesame oil (15 ml)

1 tbsp. brown sugar (12.5 g)

2 tsp. cornstarch (5 g)

Cooking:

In a wok, combine all ingredients apart from the cornstarch. Stir over medium heat until well mixed. Make a slurry with cornstarch and a little water, then stir into the sauce. Continue to cook, stirring until the sauce thickens. Enjoy!

5. Perfect Peanut Sauce

(4 servings, 190 kcal/serving, Cooking time: 10 minutes, Proteins: 6g, Fats: 16g, Carbs: 7g)

Ingredients:

1/2 cup peanut butter (120 g)
1/4 cup soy sauce (60 ml)
2 tbsp. lime juice (30 ml)
2 tbsp. brown sugar (25 g)
1/2 tsp. crushed red pepper flakes (1 g)

Cooking:

Assemble all the ingredients in your wok. Over medium heat, stir them together until the mixture is smooth. Keep it warm but ensure it does not bubble over. Enjoy your cooking!

6. Ginger Garlic Goodness

(4 servings, 40 kcal/serving, Cooking time: 10 minutes, Proteins: 1g, Fats: 1g, Carbs: 7g)

Ingredients:

1/4 cup soy sauce (60 ml)
1/4 cup water (60 ml)
1 tbsp. minced fresh ginger (6 g)
2 cloves garlic, minced (6 g)
1 tbsp. honey (21 g)
1 tbsp. cornstarch (8 g)

Cooking:

Gather all ingredients except cornstarch in your wok and heat on medium. Meanwhile, dissolve cornstarch in water. Add this to the wok and stir until sauce thickens. Enjoy your cooking!

7. Sweet Spicy Soy

(4 servings, 70 kcal/serving, Cooking time: 15 minutes, Proteins: 2g, Fats: 0g, Carbs: 17g)

<u>Ingredients</u>:

1/3 cup low sodium soy sauce (80 ml)

1/4 cup honey (85 g)

1/4 cup water (60 ml)

2 tbsp. rice vinegar (30 ml)

1 tbsp. minced garlic (6 g)

1 tbsp. sambal oelek or other chili paste (15 g)

2 tsp. cornstarch (5 g)

<u>Cooking</u>:

In your wok, combine soy sauce, honey, water, rice vinegar, minced garlic, and chili paste, and bring to a simmer. Dissolve cornstarch in a little cold water, then add to the wok, stirring until the sauce thickens. Enjoy your cooking!

---

8. Basic Curry Sauce

(4 servings, 130 kcal/serving, Cooking time: 25 minutes, Proteins: 2g, Fats: 9g, Carbs: 12g)

<u>Ingredients</u>:

1 medium onion, finely chopped (110 g)

2 cloves of garlic, minced (6 g)

1 tbsp. fresh ginger, grated (6 g)

2 tbsp. vegetable oil (30 ml)

2 tbsp. curry powder (12 g)

1 cup canned tomatoes, crushed (240 ml)

1 cup coconut milk (240 ml)

1 tbsp. low sodium soy sauce (15 ml)

Salt to taste

1 tsp. cornstarch (3 g)

<u>Cooking</u>:

Sauté chopped onion, minced garlic, and grated ginger in oil. Stir in curry powder. Add crushed tomatoes, coconut milk, soy sauce; simmer for 15-20 minutes. Thicken with cornstarch in cold water. Salt to taste. Done!

9. Tangy Sesame Soy

(4 servings, 70 kcal/serving, Cooking time: 10 minutes, Proteins: 1g, Fats: 3g, Carbs: 9g)

Ingredients:

1/3 cup low sodium soy sauce (80 ml)

1/4 cup water (60 ml)

2 tbsp. rice vinegar (30 ml)

1 tbsp. sesame oil (14 ml)

1 tbsp. brown sugar (13 g)

1 tbsp. toasted sesame seeds (9 g)

1 tsp. cornstarch (3 g)

Cooking:

Combine all ingredients except cornstarch and sesame seeds in your wok and bring to a simmer. Dissolve cornstarch in a little cold water and add to the wok, stirring until the sauce thickens. Sprinkle in the toasted sesame seeds just before serving. Enjoy!

10. Spicy Black Bean Blast

(4 servings, 60 kcal/serving, Cooking time: 15 minutes, Proteins: 2g, Fats: 1g, Carbs: 11g)

Ingredients:

1/4 cup low sodium soy sauce (60 ml)

1/4 cup black bean sauce (60 ml)

1/4 cup water (60 ml)

2 tbsp. rice vinegar (30 ml)

1 tbsp. chili flakes (6 g)

1 clove garlic, minced (3 g)

1 tsp. cornstarch (3 g)

Cooking:

Combine all ingredients except cornstarch in your wok and heat to a simmer. In a separate bowl, dissolve cornstarch in a little cold water, then add to the wok. Stir until the sauce has thickened. Enjoy!

11. Marvelous Miso Soy

(4 servings, 75 kcal/serving,
Cooking time: 15 minutes, Proteins:
3g, Fats: 1g, Carbs: 13g)
Ingredients:
1/3 cup soy sauce (80 ml)
2 tbsp. white miso paste (30 g)
1/4 cup water (60 ml)
2 tbsp. mirin (30 ml)
1 tbsp. sugar (13 g)
1 tsp. cornstarch (3 g)
Cooking:
In your wok, combine soy sauce,
miso paste, water, mirin, and sugar.
Heat on medium, stirring until the
miso and sugar is fully dissolved. In
a separate bowl, dissolve the
cornstarch in a little water, then add
to the wok. Stir until the sauce
thickens. Enjoy your cooking!

12. Cozy Coconut Sauce

(4 servings, 100 kcal/serving, Cooking time: 15
minutes, Proteins: 1g, Fats: 8g, Carbs: 8g)
Ingredients:
1 can of coconut milk (400 ml)
2 cloves garlic, minced (6 g)
1 small chili pepper (15 g)
1 tbsp. fresh lime juice (15 ml)
1 tbsp. soy sauce (15 ml)
1 tsp cornstarch (3 g)
Salt to taste
Cooking:
Combine all ingredients except cornstarch in your
wok, and bring to a simmer.
In a separate bowl, dissolve cornstarch in a little cold
water, then add to the wok.
Stir until the sauce thickens, season with salt to
taste.
Your coconut sauce is ready! Perfect for drizzling
over grilled seafood or stir-fried vegetables. Enjoy!

13. Lemongrass Soy Twist

(4 servings, 60 kcal/serving, Cooking time: 15 minutes, Proteins: 2g, Fats: 0g, Carbs: 13g)

Ingredients:

1/3 cup low sodium soy sauce (80 ml)
1/4 cup water (60 ml)
2 tbsp. fresh lemongrass, finely chopped (20 g)
1 tbsp. brown sugar (13 g)
1 tbsp. lime juice (15 ml)
1 clove garlic, minced (3 g)
1 tsp cornstarch (3 g)

Cooking:

Combine all ingredients except cornstarch in your wok and bring to a simmer. In a separate bowl, dissolve cornstarch in a little cold water, then add to the wok, stirring until the sauce has thickened. Enjoy!

14. Umami Mushroom Elixir

(4 servings, 45 kcal/serving, Cooking time: 20 minutes, Proteins: 2g, Fats: 1g, Carbs: 8g)

Ingredients:

1/3 cup soy sauce (80 ml)
1/4 cup water (60 ml)
1 cup finely chopped mushrooms (70 g)
1 clove garlic, minced (3 g)
1 tbsp. rice vinegar (15 ml)
1 tsp. cornstarch (3 g)

Cooking:

In your wok, combine soy sauce, water, mushrooms, garlic, and rice vinegar. Bring to a simmer and let it cook for about 10 minutes to allow the mushroom flavors to infuse the sauce. Dissolve cornstarch in a little cold water, then add to the wok, stirring until the sauce thickens. Enjoy!

15. Coconut Mango Mix

(4 servings, 120 kcal/serving, Cooking time: 25 minutes, Proteins: 1g, Fats: 6g, Carbs: 18g)

Ingredients:

1 ripe mango (200 g)
1/2 cup coconut milk (120 ml)
1 tbsp. fresh lime juice (15 ml)
1 tbsp. low sodium soy sauce (15 ml)
1 tbsp. brown sugar (13 g)
1 small chili pepper (15 g)
1 tsp cornstarch (3 g)

Cooking:

In a blender, puree the mango until smooth. Set aside. In your wok, combine the mango puree, coconut milk, lime juice, soy sauce, brown sugar, and chopped chili pepper. Bring the mixture to a simmer over medium heat. In a small bowl, dissolve the cornstarch in a little cold water, then add it to the wok. Stir the sauce continuously until it thickens.   Remove the sauce from the heat and let it cool before using it in your recipes. This sauce is perfect for drizzling over grilled seafood, chicken, or stir-fried vegetables.

Chapter 13. Gluten-Free Goodness

1.GF Shrimp and Snow Pea Wok
(servings, 280 kcal/serving, Cooking time: 20 minutes, Proteins: 23g, Fats: 9g, Carbs: 24g)
Ingredients:
1 lb. shrimp (454 g)
2 cups snow peas (160 g)
2 cloves garlic, minced (6 g)
2 tbsp. gluten-free soy sauce (30 ml)
1 tbsp. sesame oil (14 g)
Cooking:
Warm the sesame oil over medium heat in your WOK. Add shrimp, and stir-fry until they turn pink around 4-5 minutes. Add garlic and snow peas, and stir-fry for 3-4 minutes. Drizzle with gluten-free soy sauce, stir well and serve. Enjoy this light, nutritious dish!

2. GF Chicken and Pepper Stir-Fry
(4 servings, 350 kcal/serving, Cooking time: 25 minutes, Proteins: 35g, Fats: 15g, Carbs: 15g)
Ingredients:
1 lb. chicken breast (454 g)
2 bell peppers (300 g)
1 onion (200 g)
2 tbsp. gluten-free soy sauce (30 ml)
1 tbsp. olive oil (14 g)
Cooking:
Warm the sesame oil over medium heat in your WOK. Add chicken, and sauté until cooked through (about 5-7 minutes).
Add onion and bell peppers, and sauté until softened (about 3-5 minutes). Stir in soy sauce, mix well and serve. Enjoy your meal!

3. GF Veggie and Tofu Stir-Fry

(4 servings, 300 kcal/serving, Cooking time: 30 minutes, Proteins: 18g, Fats: 15g, Carbs: 25g)

Ingredients:

1 lb. firm tofu (454 g)

2 cups mixed vegetables (300 g)

2 tbsp. gluten-free soy sauce (30 ml)

1 tbsp. coconut oil (14 g)

Cooking:

Heat wok on medium, add coconut oilю.

Add tofu, sear until golden (5-7 mins).

Add mixed vegetables, sauté until tender (3-5 mins). Drizzle with soy sauce, toss to combine, and serve. Enjoy!

4. GF Beef and Broccoli Wok

(4 servings, 370 kcal/serving, Cooking time: 20 minutes, Proteins: 35g, Fats: 20g, Carbs: 15g)

Ingredients:

1 lb. beef steak, thinly sliced (454 g)

1 head of broccoli (184 g)

2 cloves garlic, minced (6 g)

2 tbsp. gluten-free soy sauce (30 ml)

1 tbsp. vegetable oil (14 g)

Cooking:

Heat WOK on medium, and add vegetable oil. Add beef, and stir-fry until browned (4-6 mins).

Stir in garlic, broccoli, and sauté until tender (3-5 mins). Finish with soy sauce, toss to combine, and serve.

5. GF Scallop and Zucchini Wok

(4 servings, 270 kcal/serving, Cooking time: 15 minutes, Proteins: 23g, Fats: 11g, Carbs: 18g)

Ingredients:

1 lb. scallops (454 g)

2 cups zucchini (300 g)

1 tbsp. butter (14 g)

2 cloves garlic, minced (6 g)

1 tbsp. lemon juice (15 ml)

Cooking:

Melt butter in the heated wok. Sauté scallops until golden (4-5 mins). Add zucchini and garlic, and stir-fry until tender (3-4 mins). Finish with a squeeze of fresh lemon juice and serve.

Enjoy your delicious and healthy meal! Enjoy

6. GF Veggie Quinoa Wok

(4 servings, 340 kcal/serving, Cooking time: 30 minutes, Proteins: 12g, Fats: 11g, Carbs: 50g)

Ingredients:

2 cups cooked quinoa (410 g)

1 cup mixed vegetables (150 g)

2 tbsp. gluten-free soy sauce (30 ml)

1 tbsp .vegetable oil (14 g)

Cooking:

Heat WOK with vegetable oil. Add pre-cooked quinoa and a mix of your favorite vegetables. Stir-fry until vegetables are tender (4-6 mins). Finish with a drizzle of soy sauce, stir to combine well. Enjoy this hearty and fiber-rich meal!

7. GF Tofu and Bok Choy Wok

(4 servings, 220 kcal/serving, Cooking time: 15 minutes, Proteins: 12g, Fats: 14g, Carbs: 12g)

Ingredients:

1 lb. firm tofu (454 g)

2 cups bok choy (140 g)

2 tbsp. gluten-free soy sauce (30 ml)

1 tbsp. vegetable oil (14 g)

Cooking:

Warm up your wok and add oil. Stir-fry tofu pieces until they achieve a golden hue (5-7 mins). Introduce bok choy to the wok and keep cooking until it wilts down (3-4 mins).

Wrap it up by adding soy sauce, stirring to spread it evenly. Enjoy this light, nutritious, and satisfying dish!

8. GF Pork and Green Bean Wok

(4 servings, 350 kcal/serving, Cooking time: 25 minutes, Proteins: 34g, Fats: 20g, Carbs: 12g)

Ingredients:

1 lb. pork loin (454 g)
2 cups green beans, trimmed (240 g)
2 tbsp. gluten-free soy sauce (30 ml)
1 tbsp. vegetable oil (14 g)

Cooking:

Heat the wok and pour in oil, allowing it to warm up. Stir-fry the pork in the heated oil until it's fully cooked (5-7 mins). Introduce the green beans into the wok, cooking them until they become crisp-tender (3-4 mins). Finish the dish by swirling in the soy sauce, ensuring it's evenly distributed. Serve hot, and enjoy this deliciously quick meal!

9. GF Mushroom and Spinach Wok

(4 servings, 240 kcal/serving, Cooking time: 15 minutes, Proteins: 6g, Fats: 20g, Carbs: 12g)

Ingredients:

1 lb. mushrooms (454 g)
2 cups spinach (60 g)
2 tbsp. gluten-free soy sauce (30 ml)
1 tbsp. vegetable oil (14 g)

Cooking:

Heat your wok over medium heat and add the oil, letting it warm up. Next, add the mushrooms to the wok and stir-fry them until they turn a nice golden color (5-7 minutes). Add the spinach to the wok and continue to stir-fry until it has wilted down (2-3 minutes). To finish, splash in the soy sauce and give everything a good stir to combine. This quick, simple, and nutritious dish is best served hot. Enjoy!

10. GF Shrimp with Asparagus Wok

(4 servings, 240 kcal/serving, Cooking time: 20 minutes, Proteins: 28g, Fats: 12g, Carbs: 8g)

Ingredients:

1 lb. shrimp (454 g)
2 cups asparagus (180 g)
2 tbsp. gluten-free soy sauce (30 ml)
1 tbsp. vegetable oil (14 g)

Cooking:

Start by heating your wok over medium heat and add the oil, letting it get warm. Add the shrimp and cook until they turn pink, which usually takes around 4-5 minutes. Add asparagus to the wok and stir-fry until they are crisp-tender; this should take about 3-4 minutes.

Lastly, swirl in the soy sauce and mix everything together. Your dish is ready to be served. Enjoy your meal!

11. GF Sweet sour Chicken Wok

(4 servings, 320 kcal/serving, Cooking time: 30 minutes, Proteins: 30g, Fats: 14g, Carbs: 20g)

Ingredients:

1 lb. chicken breast (454 g)

1/2 cup gluten-free sweet and sour sauce (125 ml)

1 tbsp. vegetable oil (14 g)

Cooking:

Start by heating your wok over medium heat and add the oil, letting it get warm. Add the chicken pieces and cook until they turn golden, which usually takes around 5-7 minutes. Pour the sweet and sour sauce over the chicken and stir for about 2-3 minutes until the chicken is well coated, and the sauce is heated through.

Your dish is ready to be served. Enjoy your meal!

---

12. GF Pesto Zucchini Noodle Wok

(4 servings, 280 kcal/serving, Cooking time: 15 minutes, Proteins: 7g, Fats: 24g, Carbs: 10g)

Ingredients:

4 medium zucchinis (908 g)

1/4 cup gluten-free pesto (60 g)

1 tbsp. vegetable oil (14 g)

Cooking:

Heat oil in WOK (2 mins).Stir-fry zucchini noodles until tender (3-5 mins). Mix in pesto.Your dish is ready to be served. Enjoy your meal!

13. GF Shrimp and Snap Pea Wok

(4 servings, 320 kcal/serving, Cooking time: 25 minutes, Proteins: 32g, Fats: 16g, Carbs: 15g)

Ingredients:

1 lb. shrimp, peeled and deveined (454 g)
2 cups snap peas (256 g)
2 tbsp. gluten-free soy sauce (30 ml)
1 tbsp. vegetable oil (14 g)

Cooking:

Start by heating your wok over medium heat. Add oil and allow it to warm for about 2 minutes. Introduce the zucchini noodles to the wok and sauté them until they become tender. This usually takes about 3-5 minutes. Mix in the pesto, ensuring that the noodles are well coated.

Your Zucchini Noodles with Pesto are now ready to be enjoyed!

14. GF Cauliflower Rice Wok

(4 servings, 150 kcal/serving, Cooking time: 20 minutes, Proteins: 6g, Fats: 8g, Carbs: 16g)

Ingredients:

3 heads of cauliflower, riced (588 g)
1 tbsp. vegetable oil (14 g)
Salt to taste

Cooking:

Begin by heating your wok over medium heat. Add oil and let it heat for about 1-2 minutes. Add the cauliflower rice to the wok and stir-fry it until it's tender. This process will take approximately 5-7 minutes. Season with salt and stir well for about 1 minute.

Your stir-fried cauliflower rice is ready to serve! Enjoy this healthy and low-carb dish!

15. GF Honey Lime Chicken Wok

(4 servings, 365 kcal/serving, Cooking time: 30 minutes, Proteins: 28g, Fats: 14g, Carbs: 32g)

Ingredients:

1 lb. chicken breast (454 g)

3 tbsp. honey (63 g)

1 tbsp. lime juice (15 ml)

1 tbsp. vegetable oil (14 g)

Cooking:

Preheat your wok over medium heat with the oil (approximately 1-2 minutes). Add chicken and cook until no longer pink (about 5-7 minutes). Stir in honey and lime juice, simmering until the chicken is well-coated (another 2-3 minutes). Enjoy!

Chapter 14: Desserts

1. Banana Honey Wok

(4 servings, 310 kcal/serving, Cooking time: 15 minutes, Proteins: 2g, Fats: 14g, Carbs: 48g)
Ingredients:
4 bananas, ripe but firm (480 g)
4 tbsp. honey (85 g)
2 tbsp. vegetable oil (30 ml)
1/2 tsp. cinnamon (1.3 g)
Cooking:
Slice the bananas in half lengthwise. Warm the oil in the WOK over a medium flame. Add the bananas and fry until golden brown on each side (about 3-4 minutes per side, total 6-8 minutes). Drizzle the honey and sprinkle the cinnamon over the bananas. Stir gently to combine (about 1 minute). If you wish, you may serve this dish warm, accompanied by a scoop of your favorite ice cream. Enjoy your dessert.

2. Coconut Pineapple WOK

(4 servings, 250 kcal/serving, Cooking time: 15 minutes, Proteins: 2g, Fats: 8g, Carbs: 46g)
Ingredients:
1 pineapple (905 g)
2 tbsp. coconut oil (28 g)
1/4 cup brown sugar (50 g)
1/4 cup shredded coconut (20 g)
Cooking:
Cut the pineapple into chunks. Warm the coconut oil in the WOK over a medium flame. Add the pineapple and brown sugar. Stir fry until caramelized (about 5-7 minutes). Sprinkle with shredded coconut and serve warm. Enjoy your dessert!

3. Cherry Jubilee Flambe WOK

(4 servings, 300 kcal/serving, Cooking time: 20 minutes, Proteins: 1g, Fats: 0g, Carbs: 75g)
Ingredients:
3 cups of pitted cherries (480 g)
1 cup granulated sugar (200 g)
1/4 cup brandy (60 ml)
Vanilla ice cream for serving
Cooking:
Caramelize cherries and sugar in hot WOK (5-7 mins). Add brandy, and ignite carefully (1-2 mins). Let flame die out (2-3 mins). Serve over ice cream. Enjoy this fiery dessert, but be careful with the flame!

4. Banana Nutella WOK

(4 servings, 435 kcal/serving, Cooking time: 10 minutes, Proteins: 4g, Fats: 16g, Carbs: 70g)

Ingredients:

4 peeled bananas (480 g)

1 tbsp. butter (14 g)

4 tbsp. Nutella (80 g)

Vanilla ice cream for serving

Cooking:

Melt butter in WOK, add bananas, and stir-fry until golden (5-7 mins). Stir in Nutella until bananas are coated (2-3 mins). Serve over ice cream. Enjoy!

5. Pineapple WOK Cake

(4 servings, 355 kcal/serving, Cooking time: 40 minutes, Proteins: 4g, Fats: 14g, Carbs: 54g)

Ingredients:

2 cups flour (250 g)

1.5 cups sugar (300 g)

1/2 cup vegetable oil (120 ml)

2 eggs

2 tsp. baking soda (10 g)

Pinch of salt

20 oz. can of crushed pineapple (565 g)

Cooking:

Combine your flour, sugar, oil, eggs, baking soda, salt, and pineapple in a bowl and mix thoroughly. Pour your mixture into a greased WOK and cover with a lid. Let the dish simmer on low heat for around 30 minutes.

Allow to cool before serving this delightful Pineapple Wok Cake. Enjoy!

6. Chocolate Marshmallow WOK

(4 servings, 365 kcal/serving, Cooking time: 20 minutes, Proteins: 3g, Fats: 15g, Carbs: 57g)

Ingredients:

1 cup milk chocolate (200 g)
1.5 cups mini marshmallows (200 g)
100 g digestive biscuits
50 g butter (melted))

Cooking:

Line wok with foil, layer bottom with biscuits (2-3 mins). Place chocolate, marshmallows, and butter in WOK, and cover (1 min). Stir occasionally until melted and mixed (8-10 mins). Allow to cool. Enjoy your wok-made s'mores!

7. WOK Pear Tarte Tatin

(4 servings, 345 kcal/serving, Cooking time: 50 minutes, Proteins: 3g, Fats: 18g, Carbs: 47g)

Ingredients:

4 pears, peeled and cored (about 800 g)
1/2 cup granulated sugar (100 g)
1/4 cup butter (50 g)
1 sheet puff pastry

Cooking:

Melt the sugar in the wok until it becomes caramel. Stir in the butter. Arrange the pears in the wok, cut side up. Cover with a sheet of puff pastry, tucking the edges down the side of the WOK. Place a lid on the WOK and allow it to cook on a low flame for roughly 30 minutes. To serve, carefully invert the tarte onto a serving plate. Enjoy this French classic right from your WOK!

8. Caramelized Banana Wok

(4 servings, 260 kcal/serving, Cooking time: 10 minutes, Proteins: 2g, Fats: 8g, Carbs: 52g)

Ingredients:

4 bananas (600 g)

2 tbsp butter (28 g)

1/4 cup brown sugar (55 g)

Cooking:

Slice bananas into thick coins. In a wok, melt the butter over medium heat. This process should take about 1-2 minutes.

Add bananas and brown sugar, and stir-fry until tender and caramelized (4-6 mins). Serve warm with a scoop of ice cream. Enjoy!

9. Blueberry Lemon Wok Pancakes

(4 servings, 245 kcal/serving, Cooking time: 30 minutes, Proteins: 5g, Fats: 9g, Carbs: 37g)

Ingredients:

1 cup all-purpose flour (120 g)

1 tbsp. sugar (12.5 g)

1 tsp. baking powder (5 g)

1/2 tsp. baking soda (2.5 g)

1/4 tsp. salt (1.5 g)

1 cup buttermilk (240 g)

1 large egg (50 g)

2 tbsp. butter melted (28 g)

1 cup blueberries (150 g)

Zest of 1 lemon

Cooking:

In a large bowl, combine flour, sugar, baking powder, baking soda, and salt. In another bowl, whisk together the buttermilk, egg, and melted butter. Pour the wet mixture into the dry one and stir until they are just combined. Fold in blueberries and lemon zest (2-3 mins).Heat wok over medium heat, lightly oil. Pour 1/4 cup batter for each pancake, cook until bubbles appear, flip and cook until golden (2-3 mins per pancake). Repeat with the remaining batter (depending on the number of pancakes). Serve warm with a drizzle of maple syrup. Enjoy these fluffy, fruit-filled pancakes!

10. Apple Crumble WOK

(4 servings, 335 kcal/serving, Cooking time: 45 minutes, Proteins: 3g, Fats: 15g, Carbs: 49g)

Ingredients:

4 apples, peeled, cored, and sliced (720 g)

1/2 cup brown sugar, divided (110 g)

1/2 cup flour, divided (60 g)

1/2 cup oats (50 g)

1/2 cup butter, cubed and chilled (113 g)

1/2 tsp. cinnamon (1.3 g)

Cooking:

Preheat your WOK over medium heat. Add the sliced apples, half of the brown sugar, and half of the flour, then stir until the apples are coated. In a different bowl, mix the oats, the remaining sugar, the remaining flour, and cinnamon together. Blend the chilled butter into this mixture until it takes on a coarse, crumbly texture. Sprinkle this oat mixture over the apples that are in the wok.

Cover and cook over medium-low heat for about 30 minutes or until the apples are tender and the topping is golden. Serve your apple crumble warm with a scoop of vanilla ice cream. Enjoy!

11. Banana Chocolate Flambe WOK

(4 servings, 400 kcal/serving, Cooking time: 15 minutes, Proteins: 4g, Fats: 15g, Carbs: 65g)

Ingredients:

2 bananas, sliced (240 g)

2 tbsp. unsalted butter (28 g)

1/4 cup dark rum (60 ml)

1/4 cup brown sugar (55 g)

1/2 cup dark chocolate, chopped (88 g)

Cooking:

Melt butter in a hot WOK, stir in brown sugar until it melts (3-4 mins).

Add banana slices and gently brown (2-3 mins). Pour in rum, then ignite carefully (1-2 mins, but please be super careful). As the flame dies out, scatter dark chocolate over bananas and let it melt (2-3 mins). Serve right away, optionally with a scoop of vanilla ice cream. Enjoy!

12. Honey Thyme Grilled Peaches Wok

(4 servings, 180 kcal/serving, Cooking time: 15 minutes, Proteins: 1g, Fats: 0g, Carbs: 47g)

Ingredients:

4 peaches, halved and pitted (600 g)

2 tbsp. honey (42 g)

4 sprigs of fresh thyme

Cooking:

Heat your WOK on medium (1-2 mins). Sear peaches cut side down until grill marks appear (4-5 mins). Drizzle with honey, add a thyme sprig to each half, and let the heat infuse the thyme aroma (2-3 mins). Serve warm. Enjoy!

13. Almond Pear Wok

(4 servings, 225 kcal/serving, Cooking time: 15 minutes, Proteins: 3g, Fats: 9g, Carbs: 36g)

Ingredients:

7 pears, peeled and sliced (600 g)

2 tbsp. butter (28 g)

2 tbsp. brown sugar (25 g)

1/4 cup sliced almonds (35 g)

Cooking:

Melt butter in a hot WOK. Toss in the pears and sugar, and stir-fry until the fruit softens (4-6 mins). Scatter almonds over the pears, toasting them lightly (2-3 mins). Serve warm. Enjoy!

14. Balsamic Caramelized Fig Wok

(4 servings, 210 kcal/serving, Cooking time: 15 minutes, Proteins: 1g, Fats: 0g, Carbs: 54g)

Ingredients:

12 fresh figs, halved (600 g)

1/2 cup sugar (100 g)

1/4 cup balsamic vinegar (60 ml)

Cooking:

Melt sugar into caramel in a heated WOK (5-7 mins). Lay the figs in the caramel, cut side down, and cook until caramelized (3-5 mins). Flip, drizzle with balsamic vinegar, and reduce to a syrupy consistency (2-3 mins). Serve warm. Enjoy!

15. Lime Mango Wok

(4 servings, 220 kcal/serving, Cooking time: 10 minutes, Proteins: 2g, Fats: 1g, Carbs: 55g)

<u>Ingredients</u>:

2 mangoes, peeled and sliced (600 g)

2 tbsp. honey (42 g)

Juice of 1 lime (30 ml)

<u>Cooking</u>:

Add mango slices to the sizzling WOK. Drizzle honey and stir-fry until caramelized (5-7 mins).Splash lime juice for a tangy touch. Serve warm. Enjoy!

Chapter 15: Conclusion

Ladies and gents, culinary wanderers and flavor fanatics, can you believe it? Here we are, tiptoeing on the brink of the grand finale of our gastronomic escapade – the marvelous Wok Chronicles! Join me, with excitement bubbling in our hearts and curiosity sizzling in our souls, as we unearth the wisdom and wonders from our exhilarating plunge into the enigmatic world of the wok.

We embarked on a whirlwind journey through time, whisking us back to ancient China, where the tale of the WOK began. We danced with delight, unearthing its captivating history – from a humble grain dryer to a symbol of culture and culinary heritage. This enchanted vessel proved to be a shape-shifting marvel, dazzling us with its spellbinding skills in stir-frying, deep-frying, boiling, steaming, and even smoking! Flavors and aromas swirled and twirled, leaving us utterly bewitched.

Oh, but the magic of the WOK doesn't end there! It's a demanding mentor, calling for an artful dance of heat management, a rhythmic beat of stirring and tossing, and a precise cadence in introducing ingredients – all culminating in the mystical "wok hei," that wondrous breath that ignites flavors with pure enchantment.

We delved deeper, uncovering its alchemical arsenal of tools – the wok spatula, a conductor's baton in our culinary symphony; the bamboo steamer, a wand weaving delightful spells of delicate dumplings and tender veggies; and the spider strainer, rescuing ingredients from bubbling oil like a heroic sorcerer.

And, oh, the ingredients! Each a mysterious elixir – soy sauce, oyster sauce, sesame oil, and cornstarch – brewing their magic potions to elevate ordinary dishes into extraordinary delights. They stirred depths of flavor and complexity in our creations, taking us on a gustatory adventure.

But beyond the surface, the WOK revealed its true essence – not just a cooking vessel but a bridge that connects us to our culinary ancestors and diverse cultures. Embodying resourcefulness, adaptability, and creativity, it speaks a universal language – the language of food that transcends all boundaries.

As you turn the final pages of this epic, carry the essence and enchantment of the WOK with you. Embrace it as a magical tool for culinary exploration, a portal to uncharted flavors, and a catalyst for joy and creativity in your kitchen. In the world of food, the possibilities are boundless – a boundless feast of exploration.

My heart brims with gratitude for each of you daring adventurers who embarked on this culinary quest. May the enchanting WOK inspire your culinary endeavors with passion and exuberance? Raise your wok spatulas high, my friends, and let's toast to the culinary artistry within us all! Bon appétit, dear comrades! May the WOK adventures never cease!